GW01418100

Effective G
Effective Schools:
Developing the Partnership

Effective Governors, Effective Schools: Developing the Partnership

Michael Creese

David Fulton Publishers

London

David Fulton Publishers Ltd
2 Barbon Close, London WC1N 3JX

First published in Great Britain by
David Fulton Publishers 1995

Note: The right of Michael Creese to be identified as the author of this work
has been asserted by him in accordance with the Copyright, Designs and
Patents Act 1988.

Copyright © Michael Creese

British Library Cataloguing in Publication Data

A catalogue record for this book is available from the British Library

ISBN 1–85346–386–8

Typeset by The Harrington Consultancy, London
Printed in Great Britain by The Cromwell Press, Melksham

Contents

Preface   vii

Foreword by Joan Sallis   ix

Introduction   1

How to Use this Book   5

1 The Role of the Governing Body   8

2 Building the Team   17

3 Governor–Staff Relationships   26

4 Managing the Work of the Governing Body   38

5 Governors and the Effective School   52

6 How Effective is your Governing Body?   69

Governing Body Development Plan Pro Forma   78

Further Reading   79

Index   83

Preface

It is impossible to list or even now to identify all of the people who have contributed to the philosophy and practical suggestions put forward in this volume. Colleagues over the years, both governors and teachers, speakers at conferences and the writers of many books and articles have all helped at different times to shape my thinking. Ideas from a wide variety of sources have been incorporated, sometimes almost subconsciously, into my model of educational management. I hope that all of them will accept this acknowledgement and my gratitude especially if they feel that they can identify within this text some seed which they may have planted.

Two individuals do however deserve special mention. Colin Bayne-Jardine, currently Principal County Inspector in Hereford and Worcester, for whom I had the great good fortune to work as his deputy when he was head of Culverhay School, Bath, opened my eyes to a whole range of possibilities and totally transformed my view of educational management. I have been equally fortunate to collaborate on a number of courses for governors and teachers with Howard Bradley OBE, Director of the University of Cambridge Institute of Education, and he has always been ready to share his ideas and expertise.

Probably no single individual in this country has done more to advance the cause of school governors than Joan Sallis. I am deeply indebted to her not only for her inspiration over many years but especially for her great generosity in writing a Foreword for this book. David Hopkins of the University of Cambridge Institute of Education has provided much encouragement and support, particularly during the period of my research into governor–teacher relationships. He read an early draft of this book and offered very positive comments, especially on the section devoted to school effectiveness. Margaret Young, Chair of Governors at Kesgrave High and Heath County Primary Schools and Chair of the Suffolk branch of the National Association of Governors and Managers (NAGM) also read a preliminary draft and made many useful suggestions. Terry Mahoney, Head of Governor and Local Management Services for Hertfordshire Education Authority, read a draft of chapter 5 and made a number of most helpful comments. Peter Earley, formerly of the National Foundation for Educational Research (NFER), and now at the Management Development Centre, The University of London Institute of Education, read the final draft and pointed out two possible improvements in the text which I was happy to make.

Finally I am glad to have this opportunity to acknowledge the assistance which I have received from John Owens, the Editorial Director of David Fulton Publishers. His patience and expertise helped to improve significantly the style of my work. I am deeply grateful to all of the individuals, named and unnamed, who have contributed in any way to this book but of course any errors or solecisms remain my own.

Michael Creese
Barningham
February 1995

Foreword

School governors often feel they are drowning in information about their responsibilities, and feel keenly the need of a firm yet kindly hand to lead them onto solid ground in their relationships with the school and each other. It is as though they are trying to learn their lines without knowing the part they play or how they relate to the rest of the characters. Sometimes even the plot eludes them. In these circumstances the scripts they learn often seem meaningless.

Nobody could offer a firmer or gentler hand than Michael Creese. He has been a headteacher and also a governor training co-ordinator in an LEA. He understands the complex processes of running a large school but he is also in the best sense 'governor-friendly'. He knows the potential of a good governing body working as a team, but he also understands the frustrations inherent in achieving it and the pretences which bedevil real progress.

Although there is still a place for the large, off-site training session in which governors from a wide variety of schools get expert help on the tasks they confront and exchange experiences with others from different areas, trainers are moving everywhere towards more whole-governing-body training. Sometimes the experience of others can help to illuminate problems and build confidence but in the end every governor has to cope with the personalities, the power games, the limited understanding and the human imperfections of one governing body in one school. It is only that group of people which holds the responsibility and together they must learn to share and jointly exercise it. Such tailor-made training is of course a heavy demand upon training resources but fortunately with the right kind of steering governing bodies can undertake a good deal of self-help and self-development. This book aims to give just enough of a guiding hand to activate that self-educative process.

The book implants very firmly the objectives of better teamwork and relationships. It then poses carefully structured questions to make the governing body think about what it is doing and develop its own ways forward. The best thing about it is that its language is not, as so often in texts for governors, just beyond the boundaries of the language people speak in the street. As Chesterton says:

> We hear men speaking for us of new laws strange and sweet
> But there is no man speaketh as we speak in the street.

The book emphasises how important it is to build teachers' trust by sharing their enthusiasms – an ordinary human relationship based on simple common objectives. To this end time must be used well: it is scarce and must be made to work for you. That means a bit of planning and a firm refusal to waste opportunities to see children at work. Michael Creese suggests different ways of planning the time shared with the school. Similarly, governors' time is too precious to be squandered in poorly planned activity. The characteristics of a good team are explored and positive models of good team behaviour laid before the reader. Meetings must be purposeful and productive. What makes them so? How can they be improved?

So much of what governors are taught misses its target. Governors cannot replicate, follow or meaningfully consent to all the processes of professional thinking, yet they can well comprehend the purposes of teaching, the principles of good school organisation and the nature of school improvement. It is all a matter of concentrating upon broad strategic intervention backed by planned and sympathetic observation. This book brings the processes of self-development back to such relevant goals and will be very welcome.

Joan Sallis

Introduction

The purpose of this book is to help governing bodies work more effectively and more closely in partnership with the staff towards the improvement of the quality of the education provided by their school.

This book is intended to help school governors explore some key aspects of their role, working either individually or, preferably, together as a governing body. It will also be of value to teachers, especially senior members of staff, in helping them to understand the role and work of the governing body more clearly and thus enabling them to work more closely in partnership with the governors. The 1986 and subsequent Education Acts have given considerably increased responsibilities to governing bodies and the balance of legal powers between governing bodies, local education authorities (LEAs) and headteachers has been changed. In the case of schools which have attained grant-maintained status, the governing body has all of the responsibilities previously carried by the LEA. These increased responsibilities mean that the way in which the governors carry out their duties can now have a significant impact upon the management of the school. Not only do governors find themselves with broader responsibilities than before, but their work is coming under greater public scrutiny, both through the annual report to, and meeting with, parents and through the reports produced by registered inspectors working for the Office for Standards in Education (OFSTED). As the programme of OFSTED inspections gets under way, we can expect the work of governing bodies to be reviewed and publicly commented upon more and more. Governors, parents and teachers need to discuss the implications of these changes and to establish how the governing body is to work with the school in this new situation.

There appears to be no generally accepted model for the way in which a governing body should fulfil its functions in the 1990s. Individual governors often appear uncertain about their role; when asked to define it, they come up with a variety of ideas, among which the belief that the key role of the governing body is to advise and support the school is widely held. Whilst this is an important part of the work of the governing body it is by no means the whole story, and support should certainly not always be unquestioning or uncritical. Teachers recognise that they have been given the task of educating children *on behalf of* the community and that, in state schools at least, they do so with public money. Teachers are aware that they cannot hold themselves accountable only to themselves or to fellow professionals for what goes on in the school and that they have to be ready and able to justify what they are doing in the name of the community to that community, as represented by the governing body and the parents.

In some parts of the teaching profession, however, there is still a tendency to resent the involvement in matters of school policy of governors, who are perceived as 'amateurs'. Where governors and teachers have not discussed their mutual roles and established where the boundary between them lies, the governing body may still be seen by the staff as largely peripheral to the real work of the school. Clearly teachers have expertise in the techniques of education and it may be difficult for non-professionals to offer advice in this area. However, this should not preclude governors and parents from contributing to the discussion about the sort of school they want, what its general aims should be and what should be the school's policies on matters like pupil behaviour. Indeed, in a number of areas – such as the determination of policy on sex education in the school – the responsibility lies very definitely with the governing body. While the headteacher remains responsible for the day-to-day management of the school, governing bodies have a very important part to play, in partnership with the staff, in setting the aims and policies of the school.

Governors are often encouraged to become involved in decisions about financial matters but they may be less likely to be involved in discussions about the curriculum. When curriculum issues arise teachers, on the one hand, are all too ready to say, 'Leave it to the professionals'; governors, on the other hand, uncertain of their ground and not necessarily well informed, are often happy to do so. And yet the provision of the curriculum – that is, the range of learning experiences provided by the school for the pupils – is the central function of the school, the very reason for its existence. If governors are totally excluded from discussions about policies and developments in this area, they are being excluded from the main business of the school.

Attitudes are not easily changed, however, and it may be some time before *all* teachers and headteachers come to recognise the validity of governors' involvement in evaluation, planning and policy-making. Some teachers, already under pressure from the demands of the National Curriculum and other changes brought about by recent legislation, still see the governing body as, at best, having little influence upon the work of the school and, at worst, as an encumbrance. Headteachers and teachers need to be helped to realise that lay governors do not constitute a threat but can contribute to the effectiveness of the school. The governing body usually contains representatives of all sections of the community with an interest in the school. Governors bring a wide range of experience and expertise into the school and should have at heart the best interests of pupils and staff. While they may be *volunteers*, governors need not be *amateurs*: well-informed and properly briefed, they can be a tremendous asset to the school. Governors who really know their schools can, for instance, help to allay parental concerns which may only be founded on rumour and half-truth. By asking appropriate questions and by acting as 'critical friends' governors can help teachers to clarify their thinking and to explore issues in depth, and in times of crisis they can offer considerable support to both staff and pupils.

Good partnerships between governors and staff which are based upon mutual trust and respect take time to build and depend upon positive attitudes in both partners. Such partnerships will only develop if governors and teachers meet frequently, though this can place an additional burden upon the volunteer governors. Evidence suggests that while many governors often visit their schools most of these visits are for meetings of the full governing body or one of its sub-groups. Unfortunately these meetings do not usually bring the governors into contact with many of the teachers. Governors would be well-advised to make sure that a proper proportion of their time spent in the school contributes to fostering the governor–teacher partnership.

Governors – usually busy people, frequently in full-time employment – often comment on the difficulty of getting time off work to visit their schools. They also mention the demands made on their time by attending meetings and reading the many documents – often long and dense – with which they are presented. Governors are often unused to the jargon and practices of the world of education and the information which they receive is largely controlled by the professionals. The staff, and in particular the headteacher, can contribute to the partnership by ensuring that there is a full range of easily accessible material available to governors, so that they may become properly informed about the work of their schools.

There may be apprehension on the part of some of the staff when a governor visits the school or enters a classroom. Governors should consider how they would feel if they were in the teacher's shoes and were visited in their workplace by someone they barely knew and about whose function they were uncertain. Tactless governors who adopt an inspectorial role (for which they are not trained) can cause a considerable amount of damage to the relationship between governors and teachers. For their part, teachers should recognise that the governors share a common interest in the good of the school and of the pupils in it. They should welcome and foster that interest so that governors become better informed and able to play their part in discussions about educational issues.

An effective governing body will be working as a team in partnership with the staff. Effective teams have common aims and if a partnership between governors and staff is to exist, they must share the same fundamental aim which is, in broad terms, to provide the best possible education, within the resources available, for *all* of the pupils in the school. In an effective school, both governors and staff will be seeking constantly to improve and develop their practice for the ultimate benefit of the children. It is hoped that this book will help governors and teachers along the road to self-improvement.

How to Use this Book

Experienced trainers will probably wish to move fairly rapidly through this section which offers one or two hints to those unused to leading or participating in training sessions with adults. The suggested outline programme at the end of the section may, however, be of assistance to both expert and novice alike. Over the past few years a considerable amount of time and money has been invested in providing training for school governors. Initially, much of this was provided at central locations and governors from all the schools in the area were invited to attend. While this method has had the advantage of enabling governors from different schools to meet and exchange ideas, it has only reached a relatively small proportion of the governor population. More recently, there has been a trend towards providing whole-governing-body training sessions; that is, providing an individual training session for all the governors of one school on a topic of their choice. Such sessions are usually held at the school at a time convenient to the governors, and they have the great advantage of involving a much higher proportion of governors. Training as a whole governing body also has considerable value as a team-building exercise, addressing the issues which are seen as of immediate importance to their school. However, while effective, this sort of provision can place heavy demands upon the governor-trainers from local education authorities – demands which they may not always be able to meet. There is no reason, however, why headteachers, senior staff and experienced governors should not lead some of these training sessions, particularly if appropriate materials and support are provided. It is hoped that this book will be found helpful by those leading such whole-governing-body training sessions.

Each of the following chapters includes a number of tasks which may either be undertaken by governors and teachers as individuals, or by groups of governors or teachers. Ideally, however, since this book emphasises the importance of the governor–teacher partnership, governors and some or all of the staff will work together on the tasks. Working through these exercises together will of itself help towards the development of shared understanding between the participants. Depending upon the size of the governing body and of the staff, it may be practicable to involve everyone together in one group, or it may be necessary to break up into smaller groups and then pool ideas afterwards. Once a discussion group gets larger than eight or nine people, it is very difficult for everyone to contribute in a meaningful way. Some of the tasks may be delegated to a small sub-group which could undertake the task and then report back to the whole of the governing body and/or staff.

A flip-chart is a most useful piece of equipment when working in small discussion groups of the type being recommended here. Ideas can be jotted down on the chart as they emerge for all to see, helping to stimulate people's thinking, as well as ensuring that valuable suggestions do not get forgotten. This procedure is infinitely preferable to someone making notes on a piece of A4 paper which other members of the group cannot read. Flip-chart pads are quite cheap but the stands are relatively expensive. It may be possible to borrow one or, failing that, some of the governors' training budget might be spent on the purchase of a stand, which would soon become invaluable for other meetings. It is of course possible to use the 'old-fashioned' blackboard instead of a flip-chart, but the flip-chart pad has the advantage of providing a permanent record of the points made which can, if required, be written up and circulated afterwards.

A useful way of starting several of the tasks in this book is to begin with what is known as a 'brainstorm'. This simply involves collecting together all the ideas from members of the group. Initially, ideas should not be discussed or explained but simply written up on the flip-chart as they occur to members of the group. Ideas should certainly not be discarded or discounted because they seem impracticable or 'far-out' – indeed coming up with new and possibly radical approaches should be positively encouraged. After between five and ten minutes, when the flow of ideas is flagging, discussion and explanations can begin. At this stage, some of the original ideas may be discarded, new ideas put forward, earlier ideas modified and developed, ideas grouped together, or priorities begin to emerge.

The chapters are arranged in a logical sequence and the governors and staff of a school could work through the whole book from start to finish. Alternatively, they could select the chapters which were felt to be of most immediate importance to them and work through these first. It is strongly recommended, however, that every governing body, together with some or all of the staff, should begin by working through chapter 1 because agreement upon the role of the governing body is the foundation for all that follows. The two Tasks in this chapter could be completed in just over an hour. Chapter 2 on team-building can usefully be worked through at any time by any group within the school, whether of governors or staff. Below is an outline programme which sets out one way in which the Tasks might be approached. All modules except one last about 75 minutes and they may be taken as individual events or grouped together as the basis of longer training sessions.

If, in the last resort, new governors have to take up their duties without the benefit of appropriate group training, they may find reading this book a useful 'way in'. Some of the Tasks lend themselves to this mode of access, but there is no real substitute for group work, under the supervision of an experienced and motivated leader.

One possible way of grouping the Tasks into a coherent programme

Module 1   The role of the governing body
Tasks 1.1 and 1.2

Module 2   Building the Team
Tasks 2.1, 2.2 and 2.3
Task 3.1 could be undertaken before Module 3

Module 3   Governor–Staff Relationships
Tasks 3.2, 3.3 and 3.4

Module 4   The work of the governing body
Tasks 4.1, 4.2, 4.4 and possibly 3.5

Module 5   Effective Schools
Tasks 5.1 and 5.2
Task 5.3 could be undertaken between Modules 5 and 6

Module 6   How effective is our school?
Tasks 5.4, 5.5 and 5.6

Module 7   School Development Planning
Tasks 5.7, 5.8 and 5.9

Module 8   How effective is our governing body? (This module will take about two hours)
Either Tasks 6.1, 6.2, 6.3 and 6.4 **or** use the sheets provided in chapter 6.

CHAPTER 1

The Role of the Governing Body

There are no nationally agreed guidelines to reconcile the overall legal responsibilities of governors and heads with the need for the head to have clear responsibility for managing the school on a day to day basis. Each school must reach its own agreement.

(Good Management in Small Schools, DFE 1993)

By establishing the role of the governing body, this chapter lays the foundation for all that follows. The legal responsibilities of the governing body are clear and well-defined but there is much less certainty about how governing bodies should operate and where the boundary should be between the work of the governors and the work of the headteacher and staff of the school. The headteacher is clearly responsible to the governors for the day-to-day management of the school and governors should in no way attempt to interfere in this. Governors and heads need to work out together the division of their broader responsibilities on the basis of a genuine partnership and to clarify their mutual roles so that misunderstandings are avoided. This chapter offers one way of defining the role of the governing body in a school.

Why does the role of the governing body need definition?

The legal responsibilities of governing bodies are set out in various Education Acts from 1944 onwards. *School Governors: A Guide to the Law,* published by the Department for Education (DFE), provides an easily accessible summary of the legislation. This useful booklet is regularly revised to take account of new legislation and every governor should have an up-to-date copy. Study of this Guide will show that the governing body has wide responsibilities including, for example, determining how the money provided by the LEA to run the school is to be spent, deciding on staff numbers and appointments and preparing an annual report to parents on the work of the governing body. It cannot be emphasised too strongly that all its powers are vested in the governing body *as a whole* and that individual governors have no power to act unless they have received specific delegated authority from the whole governing body. Even the Chair may only take action without the prior approval of the governing body in an emergency – for instance in the case of serious damage to the building, when to delay in order to call a full meeting would clearly not be in the best interests of the school. After taking such action, the Chair should ensure that the other governors are informed as soon as possible and that, if necessary, an emergency meeting of the governing body is convened in order to confirm the Chair's action.

While the responsibilities themselves may be clearly stated, far harder to define is what governors are actually to *do* in carrying them out. Nor is the dividing line between the responsibilities of the governing body and those of the headteacher and staff clearly established. There is no nationally agreed statement on the position of that boundary, and it is for every governing body to discuss with the headteacher and staff how they may best fulfil their mutual roles. A governing body is required, at the very least, to fulfil its legal responsibilities and this means that governors will have to take decisions, using appropriate decision-making mechanisms in which all governors have a voice and through which they are able to explore a range of options. For this to be possible a full spread of information about the school and the matters under discussion should be provided by the headteacher and staff. Schools where this is not the situation have rightly been criticised in reports produced by the OFSTED inspectors.

The degree of governors' involvement in the decision-making process is very closely linked to the state of the relationship between the governors and the staff of the school. The *effective* governing body is one which is working in partnership with the staff of the school towards a common set of aims.

The constituents of an effective partnership

Effective partnerships are best grounded in:

- Mutual trust, reliance and respect between the partners
- A clear definition of roles
- Promotion of the partnership rather than of individuals
- Sharing the risks.

If the partnership is to develop successfully governors and staff need to meet together frequently. In all but the very smallest schools, where informal contacts may be sufficient, there will be a variety of deliberate strategies through which governors and teachers are brought together. The process of building the partnership will take time and, as staff and governors leave and are replaced by newcomers, the partnership needs to be continuously rebuilt.

Defining the role of the governing body

Task 1.1 invites participants to come up with definitions of the role of the governing body 'off the top of their heads' and then, as a group, to structure their findings.

TASK 1.1 THE ROLE OF THE GOVERNING BODY (1)
This Task can be carried out by individual governors and teachers, by groups of governors or by governors and staff together. It should take about half an hour.

Begin by individually writing down half a dozen or so words or phrases which describe what in your opinion a governing body actually does. Single words should all be verbs and every phrase should contain a verb. After about five minutes individuals could combine together to form pairs and could then compare their ideas, reducing their combined set of words and phrases to six or seven. If the group is very large the pairs could then combine to form fours and repeat the process. Finally all the words and phrases from the pairs or fours are put up on the flip-chart. There will almost certainly be some duplication and it may be possible to link some of the ideas together. The group should arrive at an agreed summary before reading the rest of this chapter.

It is hoped that the list of words and statements resulting from Task 1.1 will include some of the ideas that follow.

Knowing the school

It would seem obvious that the first duty of a governor is to get to know the school of which he or she is a governor. Governors now have a wide range of legal responsibilities and are required to make decisions on many topics affecting the future of their schools, sometimes with far-reaching consequences. Without a sound and detailed knowledge of the school, it is difficult to see how such decisions can be taken properly. Visiting the school regularly will directly and indirectly help to foster good governor–teacher relationships by establishing the necessary atmosphere of mutual trust and respect. Governors are volunteers who generally have only a limited amount of time which they are able to devote to the school and they need to consider carefully how that time may best be used in order to ensure that they see the school at work. Governors who visit the school only for governors' meetings and for formal school functions are failing to obtain this fully rounded view of the school. Governors' visits to their school will be discussed in more detail in chapter 3.

Advising and supporting the staff

Governors should be in a position to offer advice and support to the staff, bringing to the school a wide range of experience and expertise. They may have knowledge from their work which can be of assistance to the school and they may have particular hobbies or interests which can be used to benefit and broaden the pupils' education. Governors also bring a fresh eye and a more detached viewpoint than the staff, who may be too close to a problem and unable to see the broader implications of a decision. When making appointments, for instance, governors can often give helpful views about the suitability or otherwise of the candidates from a perspective different to that of the education professionals. Governors may be able to advise on how a proposed policy or course of action such as a change in homework policy or an increase in class size will be seen from outside the school. Governing bodies and individual governors ought, however, to be aware of the possible implications of accepting free 'professional' advice from, say, a solicitor or an accountant who happens to be a governor. Unless the governor were properly insured the governing body might find itself in serious difficulty if it acted upon such advice which was later found to be defective. In any case, one might ask whether it is fair to the individual governor to expect him or her to give free professional advice just because s/he happens to be a governor.

Supporting the staff, particularly when the going gets tough or when a crisis hits the school, can be very important. A word or a small gesture of appreciation from a governor can work wonders for staff morale. Apparently trivial actions by governors, such as making tea for the staff at a busy parents' evening or helping the staff to clear up after the school has been broken into, can have a tremendous impact upon governor–staff relationships. Such gestures will be particularly appreciated at the end of a busy term or when there has been a period of particular stress for the staff such as an OFSTED inspection. Should the school have the misfortune to be involved in a major incident (the death of a pupil in an accident, for instance) governors, and particularly the Chair, can play a vital role in offering support and reassurance to both staff and pupils.

Operating as an effective team

Good teamwork amongst the staff of the school is essential for success and it is equally important that the governing body operates as an effective team. A good governing body is one which is clear about its purpose and in which the governors have shared values and goals. These goals are not to be confused with the aims of the school but are of course linked to them. Ideally there will be a balanced set of members of the team with a variety of skills and aptitudes – a point to be borne in mind when co-options onto the governing body are made. Support for and trust in the other team members are essential, as is openness and the ability to deal with conflict constructively. The contributions of all governors will then be valued and recognised and there will be an atmosphere at meetings which encourages debate. The important issue of team-building will be addressed in the next chapter.

Planning for the future

The major activity for the governing body comes under the broad heading of planning for the future. Good governing bodies devote their time to the discussion of key issues and do not allow themselves to become bogged down in the discussion of relatively minor matters. Planning for the future covers a wide range of activities, including governors' involvement in the school development planning process and in setting policies for the school on matters such as pupil behaviour and special educational needs. Their involvement in the production of the School Development Plan can be an expression of the importance attached by both governors and staff to this aspect of the work of the governing body. Within this Plan there could well be a sub-section – a 'Governing Body Development Plan' – which would set out areas for development and targets for the work of the governing body for the coming year. School Development Plans and the way in which governors can be involved in their preparation are discussed in more detail in chapter 5. The governing body as a whole is required to agree upon the school's budget for the forthcoming year although the detailed preparation of that budget is frequently delegated to a small group of governors or to the headteacher. The budget priorities should reflect the educational priorities set out in the School Development Plan.

The appointment of staff is a very important aspect of planning for the future of the school. Governors will often be involved in the appointment of staff, although they may choose to delegate the appointment of junior teachers and non-teaching staff to the headteacher. A strong case could be made out for the involvement of governors in almost all appointments and staff promotions both in terms of the different viewpoints which governors bring to an appointment panel and so that any possible suspicion of nepotism can be avoided. The appointment of senior staff and especially of a headteacher is probably the single most important task which a governor can be asked to undertake. No effort should be spared in order to ensure that the governors are clear precisely what experience and personal qualities they are looking for in the successful candidate. The selection process should ensure that candidates are provided with opportunities to display those qualities. At the end of the selection process the governors need to be certain that they have chosen the best possible person for the job.

Monitoring the work of the school

It is, however, not enough for the governing body merely to agree upon policies. An important part of their work will be to enquire into the operation of those policies and to ensure that there is proper monitoring of all aspects of the work of the school. There is little point in having a policy on, say, special educational needs, if there is never any enquiry into how the policy is operating and whether it is achieving its intended outcomes. The process of review needs to be continuous and planned and will form an important part of development planning within the school. The governors can work with the staff to review the work of the school, not as professional inspectors, but as 'critical friends'.

Governors will share with the staff a desire to make their school as effective as possible. Only by ascertaining, on the basis of firm evidence, where development is most needed can one begin to establish priorities for the deployment of resources. Governors and staff together engaged in the routine monitoring of that effectiveness will have an on-going and continuous awareness of the development of the school to compare with the 'snapshot' provided by the report of the latest OFSTED inspection. The governors and staff will be in a position to set the view of the inspectors against their own view of the school which has been systematically built up and is based upon evidence acquired over a period of time. An OFSTED inspection report on a school contains no surprises for a governing body or for a staff who really know their school. We shall return to this very important part of the work of the governing body in chapter 5.

Linking the school to the community

The governing body has an important part to play in linking the school to the community. Governors have a foot in both camps; they are part of the school and part of the community. They are ideally placed, therefore, to act as a channel of communication – taking messages from the school out into the community and, equally importantly, bringing messages from the community back into the school. Many schools have programmes for involving their pupils in the community in one way or another. These can include work experience schemes and work with local groups ranging from play-groups to old people's activities. Governors may be able to help to facilitate these projects through their own contacts in the community.

Communicating with parents

The governors form a very important strand in the school–parent communication system; the parent-governors are after all representative parents. It is sometimes thought that parent-governors are in some way delegates of the parents but this is not the case. Whilst they are elected by the parents, the parent-governors cannot be required by the parents to vote in a particular way. All governors are involved as far as possible in seeking the views of parents, although those governors who actually have children in the school may have more opportunities for meeting and speaking to parents. When presenting the views of parents on issues to the governing body, all governors need to be careful that they are clear just how widely held those views may be. Governors should not be unduly swayed by the views of a small, vocal group of parents.

Sometimes parents will approach a governor with a complaint about something which has happened at school. Very frequently these matters are a case of misunderstanding or are due to a breakdown in communication and almost all of them can be resolved by the parent talking to either their child's class teacher or, on issues of more general school policy, to the headteacher. The wise governor will resist the temptation to get involved at this stage and will do everything possible to encourage the parent to make a direct approach to the school. Almost all schools seek to encourage parental involvement and are open and welcoming to parents. It has to be recognised, however, that for some parents going into the school is not easy and it may be helpful in those cases for the governor to offer to accompany the parent to the school. Only if the parent, having spoken to the teacher and if necessary to the headteacher, is still dissatisfied should the governor become more involved by raising the matter with the headteacher.

The annual report from the governors to the parents and the meeting at which this report is discussed are both very important channels for establishing good communication between governors and parents. There are legal requirements about the information which the report has to contain but that does not mean that it must necessarily be dull and uninteresting. Spurred on perhaps by the annual competition organised by the *Times Educational Supplement*, some schools have gone to considerable lengths to make this important document more attractive and more readable, often including illustrations and other material provided by the pupils. The report is, however, the *governors'* report on their work and their perceptions of the school and should be seen as such. This is one report which the headteacher should not write! Unfortunately, many meetings between parents and governors have not been well attended in spite of repeated attempts to encourage parents to take part. The low attendance may be partly due to the rather formal nature of some of the meetings, with the governors seated behind a table in a rather forbidding way. Probably more discouraging is the fact that the meeting is normally to discuss what has already happened, about which little can be done. Where parents have been invited to give their views on future developments in a relaxed and informal atmosphere, perhaps with governors and parents sitting together in small groups, then attendances have been increased.

Promoting the best interests of the school

Good governors will always be concerned to promote the best interests of their schools and of education in general. In the recent past education has received some unfavourable publicity which has not always been well founded on fact. Governors who really know their schools are in an excellent position to point out to parents and members of the general public the very many good things which will be happening in their school. Teachers may be less able to do this convincingly – partly because some critics will comment, 'Well they would say that, wouldn't they!' and also because of the natural reticence of many people to speak about their own achievements. Governors ought to be able to take a pride in their school and should be ready and willing to communicate that pride to others. There are many ways in which this can be done, including of course the annual report to parents from the governing body. Links with the local media are also important and many schools have a system for communicating with the press and other media. It is perhaps appropriate to sound a note of caution here. Individual governors should be wary when asked to comment by the media on an issue and should normally refer the enquirer to either the Chair or the headteacher. Governors should certainly not make comments, even 'off-the-record', to representatives of the media without discussing the matter with either or both the Chair and the headteacher.

Here is a simple mnemonic summarising the role of the governing body:

- **Know** the school
- **Link** the school to the community
- **Advise** and support the staff
- **Plan** for the school's future
- **Promote** best interests of the school
- **Effective** teamwork
- **Monitor** the work of the school

TASK 1.2 THE ROLE OF THE GOVERNING BODY (2)

This Task complements Task 1.1 and should be undertaken by the individuals or group which carried out that Task. The discussion will probably take another half an hour or so.

Compare the statement on the role of the governing body produced by your group with the ideas set out in this chapter and make any changes that you wish.

Ensure that all staff and governors have a copy of the final agreed statement (it might perhaps form part of the school handbook or prospectus).

CHAPTER 2
Building the Team

A team is a group of people who share a common purpose and who must work together in order to achieve that purpose.

In this chapter we shall explore the nature of teamwork and seek to show both the benefits for governors (and staff) of operating as an effective team and how they can enhance their effectiveness. Governors come on to a governing body in a variety of ways – some are appointed, others elected and yet others co-opted. They come with a diversity of interests and experience but all must work together in harmony if the governing body is to be effective. It is to be hoped that, if both governors and staff are more aware of how teams develop and the types of behaviour required in a team, they will be able to work together more productively.

What is a team?

The people involved with a school can be divided up into a number of groups. There are for example the governors, the teaching staff and the non-teaching staff. These groups might be further sub-divided into, for instance, the governors' finance group, the teachers who teach, say, mathematics in the school, the school meals staff, and so on. The larger the school, the greater the number of these groups and usually the larger the membership of each. If the school is to be effective each of these groups must operate as a team and each of the teams must work together towards the fulfilment of the overall aims of the school. Working as part of a team has several advantages for both team members and for the organisation as a whole.

The benefits of effective teamwork

The benefits of effective teamwork can be summarised as follows:

18

- Help and support for team members;
- Increased commitment from team members and a sense of 'belonging';
- Improved communication and co-ordination;
- Opportunities for team members to learn from one another;
- Increased enjoyment and satisfaction for the team members.

Teams don't just happen though; a group of people brought together in a haphazard way does not automatically form itself into a team. The team has to be built, and in order to do this it is important to understand what makes an effective team. It is particularly important to give attention to team-building when new members join the team. Everyone connected with the team, in our case the school, should share a common aim. This might be stated in the most general terms as ensuring the provision of the best possible education for the pupils of the school. This very general statement is often broken down into more specific aims which may be set out in the school prospectus or brochure. Broad aims are broken down still further into more precise objectives. A school aim for instance might be to develop in the pupils lively and enquiring minds. An objective directed towards the achievement of this very broad aim might be to ensure that every pupil understood how to use the school library. In order for a school to achieve these aims, each of the groups working within the school must have its own aims and objectives, the achievement of which will contribute towards the achievement of the aims of the school.

Most schools have very good arrangements for the induction of new members of staff and governing bodies need to ensure that new members are brought into their team equally effectively. At the very least the new governor should be introduced to all of his or her colleagues on the governing body. Being introduced to a dozen or so new faces all at once can be very confusing, particularly if one is not very good at remembering names; it might be helpful to have names displayed on the table in front of governors for a meeting or two, until the newcomer has got to know everybody. Alternatively name badges worn on the lapel could be used though these can be difficult to read at a distance. The headteacher will of course invite the new governor to visit the school as soon as mutually convenient and will show him or her round and effect introductions to some or all of the staff. The new governor will often find it helpful to have a more experienced governor to act as his or her guide or 'mentor'. The mentor can meet the new governor before attending a governors' meeting for the first time to go through the agenda, explaining the educational jargon, the procedure of the meeting and the key issues which will be discussed. All new governors should be strongly encouraged to undertake some training, particularly if the LEA provides, as most do, courses specifically for newly-appointed governors.

A particular difficulty for governing bodies lies in coping with the widely varying degrees of commitment, time, expertise and training amongst its members. It is important not to confuse *quantity* of commitment with *quality* of commitment, and to recognise that governors do have other demands upon their time, some of which may vary throughout the year. It is to be hoped that all the governors will wish to play their part as fully as they are able. Encouraging individual governors to pursue their particular interests, such as finance or special educational needs, and/or to attend training events and to report back to the governing body can help them to feel that they 'belong' and are contributing to the group. A new governor joining a governing body which he or she perceives to be operating as an ineffective team is in a difficult situation. Patience and tact will be called for and the newcomer must tread carefully and try to discover the real reason for the ineffectiveness. This might be poor chairmanship, a group of governors who have failed to adjust to changed circumstances or simply governors who have not thought carefully enough about their role and how to manage their work. In such situations there may well be a small group of like-minded governors who are aware of the shortcomings and who can work together in order to effect change. A whole-governing-body training session may be an opportunity to raise some of the issues and to introduce some new working practices. Change takes time and it is better to make a successful small change rather than to attempt unsuccessfully to change everything at once.

TASK 2.1 THE CHARACTERISTICS OF AN EFFECTIVE TEAM
This Task may be undertaken either by the governors alone or by governors and teachers working together. Work in groups of between four and eight and allow exactly 25 minutes for the task.

Produce a display which will illustrate for other members of the school staff or governing body the characteristics of an effective team.

TASK 2.2 WHAT HELPED US TO WORK AS A TEAM?
This Task should be undertaken immediately after Task 2.1 and by the same group of people. It takes between 10 and 15 minutes.

After you have completed Task 2.1, spend a few minutes considering how the group was helped to achieve its goal. For example, did people make helpful suggestions? Did somebody offer to write or draw? Did members of the group offer encouragement to others? Did somebody keep an eye on the clock? Did somebody make sure that nobody felt left out or isolated? Make a list of these helpful behaviours.

Task 2.1 required the group to work as a team and Task 2.2 should have helped the group to recognise some of the behaviours which help a team to function effectively. The display could have taken a number of forms, ranging from a list of ideas on a piece of paper, through some sort of drawing or cartoon, to a dramatic presentation or even a song! No matter what the particular outcome, the team should feel pleased with it and reassured that they were able to work together in order to achieve the task in the allotted time. The individuals in the team should also try to remember the sorts of behaviours which helped them to achieve the task and consciously try to repeat and extend those behaviours when undertaking future tasks. The ideas produced by the group can now be compared with what follows.

What makes an effective team?

It follows from our definition of a team that in order to be effective as a team a governing body must have clear, agreed and common goals. No team can succeed if the players are playing towards different goals or if the players are not prepared to put the good of the team above their own self-interest. There have been many instances of sportsmen and women of great individual talent who have been ineffective team members. The common aims may not always be self-evident in the case of a governing body, with its members chosen or elected by different interest groups. A very small minority of governors may have put themselves forward for membership in order to pursue narrow personal interests which they seek to place above the interests of the group as a whole. For these reasons it is important that the governing body as a whole *does* discuss its purposes, aims and objectives and reach agreement upon them.

The composition of the ideal team

Research, particularly by Meredith Belbin (*Management Teams – Why They Succeed or Fail*, Heinemann, 1981), has shown that effective teams are made up of a variety of types of people. We are not talking here of people's occupations – accountants, architects or whatever – but rather about the way in which people behave when in a group. Eight different characters have been identified as making up an effective team:

1. A person who sets the priorities, motivates the group and gets decisions made;
2. A good organiser who can turn plans into action;
3. Someone who has plenty of ideas;
4. A good negotiator with contacts outside the team;
5. A 'challenger' who stretches the group and pushes them forward;
6. An analyst who sees all of the options and considers the outcomes carefully;
7. A listener who works well with people, particularly with difficult colleagues;
8. Someone keen on detail who keeps the group on task.

Readers with experience of working in groups may recognise some or all of these types amongst their colleagues, and the more perceptive may also be aware of the category into which they themselves fall. Ideally, a successful team needs all of these types if it is to function properly. Most individuals exhibit one dominant type of behaviour from the above list but they can also display a secondary set of characteristics, thus fulfilling two roles within the team. The ideal team consists of a minimum of four or five people and more usually eight or nine are required to ensure that each of the types identified above is present. To a large extent, however, the make-up of a governing body may be determined by factors outside the control of the group, and it may not always be possible to approach team-building in this way. Nevertheless, it can be borne in mind when co-opting new governors onto the team.

The characteristics of an effective team

Effective teams have sound procedures and good communication systems which are known to and understood by all. Procedures should cover matters such as how to place an item on the agenda, voting arrangements (if and when necessary), and the taking and prompt circulation of minutes. There is a danger where the governing body is working in sub-groups that some governors may be unaware of what decisions are being made. Nothing endangers team spirit more than the suggestion that there is an inner group within the team which is in some way more privileged than the rest of the team. Anything which smacks of this on the governing

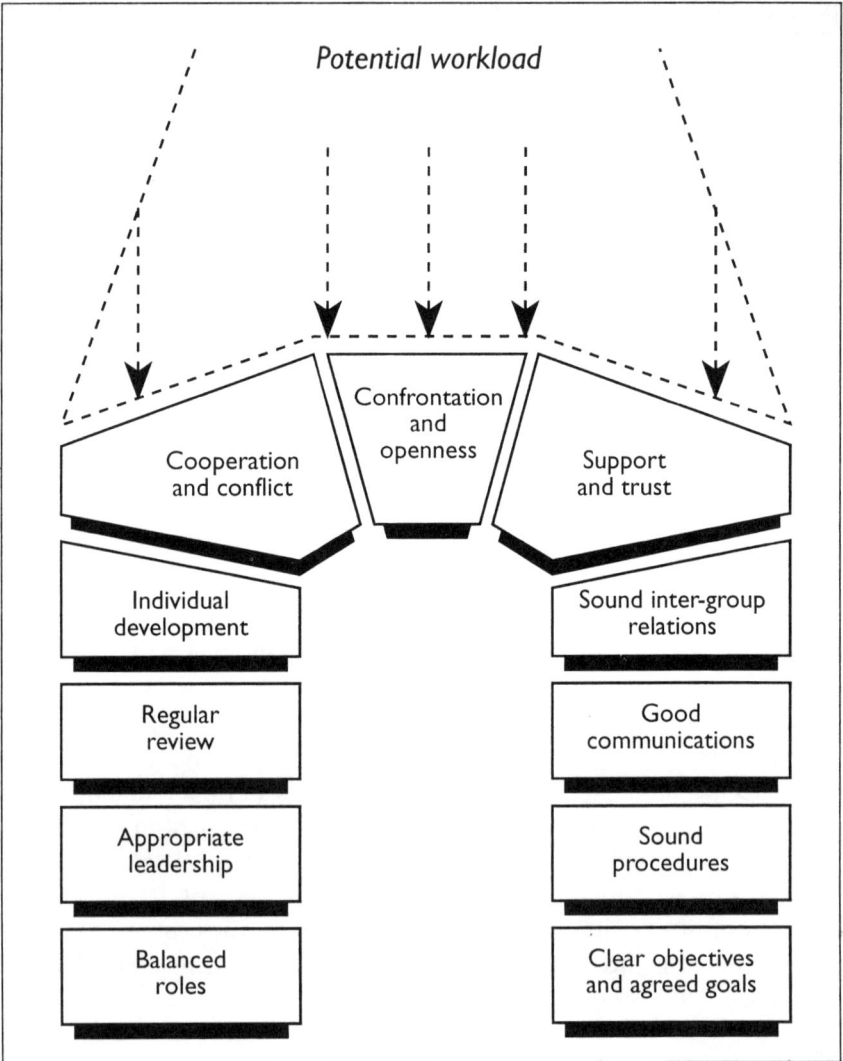

Figure 2.1: The characteristics of an effective team (from: 'Governing Bodies as Teams: why they succeed or fail. Part 1', Ann Holt and Tom Hinds. *Managing Schools Today*, **1** 1, 1991, published by Questions Publishing Company, 27 Frederick Street, Birmingham B1 3HH.)

body should be resisted at all costs. The governing body needs to develop for itself an effective and efficient communication system which will ensure that all governors are kept fully informed and that documents are promptly circulated. In a large governing body it might be helpful to organise some sort of communication 'tree' by which messages are passed along rather than having to rely upon one individual to contact every governor. Good relationships between the governing body and other groups – especially the teaching and non-teaching staff, but also including parents and others – is another important facet of team effectiveness.

An effective team is well led. Frequently on a governing body the leadership will come from the elected Chair but not always. A wise Chair will recognise when it might be more appropriate that another member of the governing body, perhaps with some specialist expertise, should provide the leadership. It *is* possible for an experienced team to function effectively without a designated leader provided that the group members have the experience, willingness and ability to ensure that the leadership functions are carried out within the group. These functions include ensuring that every member of the governing body has the opportunity to contribute to the meetings, summarising the discussions and making sure that when required clear and definite conclusions are reached. The style of leadership will be suited to the occasion. In an emergency a dynamic leader is required who can make quick decisions without wasting time. However, when something like a major organisational change is being considered, this style of leadership is likely to prove less appropriate. In such a situation the leader who consults, seeks consensus and who is able to carry his or her colleagues with him/her, will win the day.

Effective teams regularly review their operation and it should become routine that, just as the work of the school is reviewed in preparing the School Development Plan, so the governing body reviews its operations over the previous year. Were the goals which it set itself last year achieved? If not, why not? Would changes in its working methods make it more effective? Is it necessary to consider the recruitment of new governors? What are the targets for the coming year and what training and development for governors will be required?

In order to be truly effective a governing body needs to operate as a cohesive group with shared aims and values. The responsibilities are vested in the group as a whole and the work-load is too heavy to be carried by one or two individuals. It is important that contributions from all governors are equally valued and that the interests of all groups represented on the governing body are given equal respect. There can be no second-class citizens in an effective team! It is very difficult for a governing body in which one or two governors are not pulling their weight to be effective. However, it is unfair to criticise such individuals unless and until the expectations of the group have been clearly spelled out to them.

Perhaps most important of all is the way in which the governing body faces conflict and confronts difficult issues. It is all too easy, when faced with a difficult issue such as staff redundancy, to delay or attempt to avoid making a decision. Equally, it is possible to try to avoid conflict and never bring out into the open the differences which are almost certain to occur within the group from time to time. It would be most unusual if all of the governors were to be in agreement all of the time. In an effective team the members support and trust one another and are able to handle conflict openly and constructively. They work together and, moreover, they *enjoy* working together. Once a decision has been made by the governing body it must be accepted by all. It is not fair to the group for individual governors to leave the meeting and say publicly, 'The other governors decided that, but I disagree'. Collective responsibility must be maintained and, in the unlikely event of a serious disagreement on a matter of principle, the only honourable course for the dissenter may be to resign from the governing body. Clearly such drastic action should only be taken as the last resort.

TASK 2.3 HOW CAN WE MAKE OUR TEAM MORE EFFECTIVE?
This Task can be undertaken by any team within the school whether made up of governors, of staff or of a mixture of governors and staff. Allow about half an hour.

Bearing in mind the characteristics of an effective team which have been identified above, how can we make *our* team more effective?

The stages in team development

B. W. Tuckman has identified four stages in the the development of a team:

1. Forming
2. Storming
3. Norming
4. Performing

When a group of people comes together for the first time, they are naturally polite to one another, observe the social conventions and avoid committing themselves too far. Some governing bodies, perhaps because they meet so infrequently as a group, never get beyond this stage. In a team which is at this stage, there will be discussions about the nature of the task and attempts to create a structure within the team. There will often be considerable dependence upon the designated leader and complaints from team members if the leader fails to provide what they see as 'real leadership'. In the second stage of team development, group members may display very negative feelings and attempt to challenge the value of the task and the group leader. There can be considerable tension within the group with team members defensive and unwilling to take risks. If the group can get beyond this stage into the 'norming' phase there will be much more co-operation and openness and the group will begin to work more effectively together. Members will be prepared to express their feelings and views openly and will support one another and the group leader. The group which reaches the final stage of 'performing' knows where it is going and what it is trying to achieve, is confident and possesses high morale. All members of the group work hard to ensure the success of the group. [See B. W. Tuckman (1965), 'Developmental Sequences in Small Groups' in *Psychological Bulletin*, **63**, 6, published by the American Psychological Association.]

CHAPTER 3

Governor–Staff Relationships

You can't form a relationship with people you never meet.
(Primary school teacher)

There is strong evidence that differences exist in the quality of the relationship between governors and staff in different schools. Given the number of people involved, there are bound to be differences in attitudes and behaviour, and these differences are reflected in the state of the governor–staff relationship in their schools. The relationship between the governors and staff and particularly that between the governors and the headteacher is, however, crucial in determining the effectiveness of the governing body and the extent to which it is involved in the management of the school. Governors and staff together, therefore, need to consider the nature of their relationship and, if necessary, take active steps to improve it. Where there are frequent significant changes in the membership of any team, there is a corresponding need to rebuild relationships. This can be a particular problem for a governing body where governors serve a four-year term of office and therefore there can be a relatively rapid turnover of personnel. In this chapter we shall consider the factors which lead to good governor–staff relationships and discuss some practical ways of enabling governors and staff to work together more closely.

TASK 3.1 THE GOVERNOR–TEACHER RELATIONSHIP IN YOUR SCHOOL
This Task ideally should be undertaken by governors and staff working together.

Try to establish the nature of the relationship between governors and staff in your school. Be honest now!
You might approach this by means of a questionnaire which asks governors and staff to rate the state of their relationship on a six-point scale from 'Excellent' to 'Very Poor'. Other possible preliminary indicators of the state of the relationship include asking governors how many of the staff they could identify in a group photograph and *vice versa*, asking the staff how many times they met a governor during the last term or the governors how many times they visited the school last term.

Expectations

One of the most common causes of misunderstanding and friction between two groups of people is that neither group has clear and agreed expectations of the other. Sometimes, when we feel that we have been let down, we blame the other party without stopping to ask ourselves whether or not they were clear about the sort of behaviour which we expected of them. It can be very helpful for governors and staff separately to draw up a list of what each group might reasonably expect of the other. The lists can then be compared, discussed and any difficulties ironed out.

TASK 3.2 WHAT DO WE EXPECT OF ONE ANOTHER?
This is a Task in which governors and staff work in separate groups at first, before joining together. Allow 30 to 45 minutes for this activity.

Governors draw up a list of their expectations of the staff. Staff draw up a list of their expectations of the governors. Put the two lists side by side and discuss the common points and any differences. Reach an agreed statement about your expectations one of the other.

Factors which lead to good governor–teacher relationships

> **TASK 3.3 THE FACTORS WHICH LEAD TO GOOD GOVERNOR–TEACHER RELATIONSHIPS**
> *This is another Task which ideally will be undertaken by a joint group of governors and staff working together. It should take no more than 15 or 20 minutes.*
>
> List the factors which your group would identify as leading to good relationships between governors and staff.

Based on data from 68 governors and 186 teachers from eight schools, the following points have been identified as leading to good relationships between governors and teachers:

- Frequent and close contact
- Mutual understanding and respect
- Openness/honesty
- Good communication
- Trust
- Common aims
- School ethos
- Teachers also referred to the importance of 'supportive' governors.

Both staff and governors recognise frequent and close contact as a factor in establishing good governor–staff relationships. There are many opportunities for bringing governors and staff together, for instance, by involving governors in staff meetings and in-service events and by inviting staff to attend governors' meetings either as observers or to make presentations about their work. The non-teaching staff in particular may seem rather distant from the governing body and it may be helpful to co-opt a member of the non-teaching staff onto the governing body. In the majority of cases only the headteacher and the teacher-governor(s) attend governors' meetings, although the deputy head is sometimes invited as an observer. Whilst this is particularly valuable for the deputy there is no reason why it should be restricted to him or her. The deputy, who after all might well be deputising for the head on occasion, should certainly be in close touch with the governors and it is useful staff development in preparing him or her for headship. It is clear from their comments that those teachers who have been invited to a governors' meeting to talk about their work have welcomed the opportunity and found it a worthwhile experience.

In a small school it may be sufficient to depend upon the informal meetings which take place in the day-to-day operation of the school to bring governors and staff into contact. This will not be sufficient in a larger school where governors have to be enabled to meet staff in a variety of contexts so that relationships can flourish. Governors should be ready and able to devote time to meeting staff socially, at meetings and at their workplace – whether in the classroom, school kitchen or school grounds. Governors should consider carefully how they commit their available time, so that not too large a proportion is spent in meetings where staff are not present.

Teacher-governors ought to play an important part in enhancing governor–staff relationships since they know both the staff and the governors. They need not limit their role to representing teachers' views to governors and to reporting to the teachers upon the outcomes of governors' meetings. Teacher-governors can be encouraged to see the fostering of good governor–staff relationships as a key part of their role in the governing body. At the very least, teacher-governors should ensure that governors are introduced to some or all of the staff so that they can get to know one another.

Of the other factors identified by governors and staff as leading to good relationships, several – mutual understanding and respect, openness, honesty and trust – can only be built up over time and through frequent meetings. It is interesting to note that teachers look for 'supportive' governors. When talking to governors and teachers, Joan Sallis has often likened headteachers who praise their supportive governors to drunks relying on the lamp-post for propping up, whilst not seeking too much illumination! Having governors and staff who are all clear about the aims of the school and who share common values and aspirations is bound to improve their relationship. Joint discussions between governors and staff will help the development of a shared viewpoint.

A key factor in determining the nature of the governor–teacher relationship is undoubtedly the attitude of the headteacher. This is shown particularly clearly when a change of head can produce a dramatic change in the nature of the relationship. Where relationships are good, heads are open and welcoming to governors and accept and welcome their involvement in policy making. Where the head behaves in an autocratic manner or is defensive and finds communication difficult the relationship is less satisfactory. Headteachers need the ability and the willingness to communicate openly and frankly with their governors, particularly about any perceived weaknesses in the school. There is evidence to suggest that the management style adopted by the head when dealing with the governors mirrors the style which he or she adopts with the staff. Where the headteacher adopts a consultative style, he or she does so with both the governors and staff. Equally, headteachers who adopt a more autocratic management style do so with both teachers and the governing body.

Where the governors find the head unwilling to work with them in the sort of partnership which is being described, a great deal of patience, tact and diplomacy will be called for. It is important to recognise that there are no short cuts to remedying the situation. The governors should try first of all to understand the reason for the headteacher's reluctance to work more closely with them. The head may have had unfortunate experiences with governors in the past, may be unaware of the changes in the responsibilities of governing bodies brought about by recent legislation or may simply lack the confidence to share power. The governors should proceed cautiously and endeavour to persuade the head that, while they are in no way seeking to usurp his or her proper authority, they do have a role to play in the management of the school and that they are determined to play it. Above all, the governors should attempt to convince the head that they, just as much as the staff, have the best interests of the pupils at heart and wish to work *with* the headteacher and staff to make the school as effective as possible.

Governors' involvement in staff discipline

Very occasionally the governors may find themselves in the unfortunate position of having to deal with a headteacher or member of staff who is failing to perform their duties competently. Such situations are never easy but it is important to remember that the interests of the pupils in the school must come first. Where the competence of a member of staff is in question, this will normally be dealt with in the first instance by the headteacher. Only very serious instances of misconduct, such as assault or theft, will lead to instant dismissal. Where a teacher is perceived as not performing his or her duties satisfactorily both the nature of the failings and the expected areas of improvement must be made clear. A time scale for improvement may be laid down and appropriate support, which may include in-service training, must be made available. It is vital that at all stages of the process the proper procedure, as laid down in the Code on Staff Discipline and Grievance is followed. (This Code will have been formally adopted by the governing body.) Included in the procedures is the setting up of a governors' committee to deal with disciplinary matters, together with a separate appeals committee. It is essential that there is no discussion of a teacher's competence or otherwise in a full meeting of the governing body. Members of the appeals committee must be able, if required, to come to the case fresh and without any prior involvement in it. There have been occasions when the dismissal of a teacher has been successfully challenged on technical grounds, because the proper procedures were not followed. This point applies equally in the case of possible redundancy.

Enhancing governor–staff relationships

Many teachers would like to see governors more aware of what is going on in their schools, particularly in view of the responsibilities which governing bodies now have. In a survey carried out in eight schools, nearly two-thirds of the teachers would like to see governors having a greater involvement in the life and work of their schools. Teachers are particularly aware of the powers which governing bodies now have and are concerned that, when making decisions, governors should do so against a background of sound knowledge of the school and its staff and pupils. Many individual governors and governing bodies are still uncertain about their role as the constant demands which new legislation has made upon governors' time affords little space for consideration and consolidation. Teachers, too, are uncertain of the powers of governing bodies, particularly as the role of the LEA appears to be declining in matters of considerable immediate importance to the staff – for example, over pay and other personnel issues. This uncertainty cannot be good for the relationship between the two groups. While there may be disadvantages in drawing up hard and fast demarcation lines, there is certainly much to be said for a clearer delineation than currently exists.

Set out below are some suggested strategies for enhancing governor–staff relationships in schools. Many of the ideas are self-explanatory but a few merit further explanation.

- Classes 'adopting' a governor;
- Developing the role of the teacher-governor;
- More effective dissemination of proceedings of governors' meetings to staff (teaching and non-teaching);
- Governors' corner/resource area/library;
- Governors helping in classrooms/office/library/elsewhere in the school;
- Governors attending staff meetings/working groups/development planning meetings/professional development days;
- 'Governor of the month' schemes;
- Information available to staff (teaching and non-teaching) about the governors (who they are, their experience, interests, etc.);

- Inviting governors to attend school functions/trips/visits;
- Inviting governors to focus on a particular subject or event in the school;
- Greater involvement of governors in planning and evaluation in the school;
- Joint working parties of governors and teachers;
- Newsletter for governors;
- Rota visits;
- Social functions for governors and staff;
- School-based governor training;
- Staff INSET on the role of governors;
- Staff observers at governors' meetings;
- Staff presentations at governors' meetings;
- Use of governors' expertise in the school.

The idea of a class 'adopting' a governor is one way of building the relationship between a governor, a teacher and a group of children and is particularly suited to primary schools. It does assume, of course, that the number of classes in the school is greater than, or at least equal to, the number of governors excluding the head and the teacher-governor(s). To attempt to link more than one or two governors to a class in this way is probably asking too much. Ideally, each governor is linked to a different class/teacher and when the governor visits the school he or she makes a point of visiting his or her class. In this way a relationship is built up between the governor and the teacher over a period of time and the governor gets to see the children undertaking a variety of activities during the year. If things are going well the governor may maintain the link with the class or the teacher for a number of years. If the governor can only visit the school infrequently, the children may write to the governor and send samples of their work. In this case, however, it is essential that the governor responds quickly; children, especially when young, are very easily disappointed. In a secondary school, where children may be placed into different groups for different subjects rather than always being in their class group, it may be more useful to link governors to specific subject areas. This can have the further advantage of enabling governors, if they so wish, to pursue their own specialist interests and expertise.

Some schools have a 'parents' corner where parents can sit and chat to staff and where information about the school is available to them. This idea can be developed for governors. There is a considerable amount of documentation which should be available to governors. It would be inefficient to provide every governor with a copy of every publication, but it should be possible to find somewhere in the school where this material can be collected together so that it is readily available to visiting governors. One simple way of ensuring that governors receive copies of all information which is sent by the school to parents is to have a folder or envelope in the school office for each governor. Whenever a letter goes out to parents, copies are automatically placed in the folders for governors to collect when they next visit the school.

The 'governor of the month' scheme has been suggested, in conversations with governors and teachers, by Joan Sallis. The idea is that each governor in turn takes on a month and is responsible for undertaking (or finding a substitute for) all the functions requiring a governor in the school that month, whether it be presenting prizes or being involved in the appointment of a member of staff. This scheme has the virtue that busy governors can organise their diaries well in advance and can thus ensure that they will be available when required.

Some governing bodies organise governors' visits to the school on a rota. One or two governors are deputed each term to visit the school and to report back to the governing body. This system is better than no visits at all but it may make the governors' visits seem rather formal. Furthermore, on a large governing body it will be some time before each governor visits if this is the only arrangement in place. A disadvantage of both 'governor of the month' and rota systems is that they do not provide the continuity of a one-to-one link between a governor and a teacher.

TASK 3.4 ENHANCING GOVERNOR–TEACHER RELATIONSHIPS IN YOUR SCHOOL

This is another Task for a group made up of both governors and staff. Perhaps a small joint working party could be set up which would report back to the governors and staff.

Using the list of ideas set out above and any others of your own, identify three or four methods by which the state of governor–staff relationships could be enhanced in your school. Plan the implementation of those schemes.

Governors' visits to the school

It should be apparent from the discussion above that it is important for governors to visit their schools in order that the governor–teacher relationship may develop, and for them to learn about the school – what goes on there and how the children are taught. As has been indicated, governing bodies have numerous responsibilities and have to take many important decisions. These decisions can only be properly taken against a background of a real understanding of the school and how it works. However, governors should remember that they are *not* inspectors – governors visit as friends and supporters of the school, in order to gain knowledge about the school and about education in general and to become more fully integrated into the school team.

Regular visits by governors to their schools will contribute towards

- Enhancing positive relationships and trust between governors and staff;
- Helping governors become integrated into the school team;
- Helping governors gain an increased knowledge of the school, of the teaching process and of recent developments in education;
- Helping governors make informed decisions in which the staff will have confidence.

What governors need to know about their schools

There is some background information which all governors ought to know about their schools. This includes the following:

- What is the history of the school: how old is it, was it formed by an amalgamation, have there been any major changes in the organisation or type of school?
- What sort of catchment area does the school serve – inner city, leafy suburb or rural?
- How big is the school; how many pupils on roll and how many staff (teaching and non-teaching)? Is the roll rising, falling or stable? All governors should be provided with an up to date staff list.
- How is the school organised? What is the management structure?
- What are the school policies on matters such as pupil behaviour, equal opportunities, sex education, special educational needs provision?
- What is the curriculum of the school? How is the National Curriculum applied and what is the additional provision? What is the school's policy and practice on Religious Education?
- What out-of-school activities does the school offer such as clubs, musical and dramatic events, day trips and residential visits?
- What links does the school have with parents, other schools and the wider community?
- How do recent examination/test results compare with those of previous years and with those from comparable schools?
- What is the state of the school buildings and grounds?

Much of this basic background information will be found in the school's prospectus. More can be learnt through talking to the headteacher and staff. However, governors need to know much more about their schools than just the basic facts and figures. The ethos of the school – that indefinable 'feel' which defines the sort of community that the school is, how the staff treat the pupils, how the pupils treat one another, and which differentiates one school from another – cannot be learnt from studying the school prospectus.

Only by actually visiting the school and seeing it at work will governors learn what it is really like. Governors will of course visit the school for meetings, either of the full governing body or of a sub-group. Many of these meetings take place out of school time and opportunities to see the school at work may be limited. However, even on these occasions, governors can view the work displayed in classrooms. If the governors' meeting is held in a different classroom each time, governors will be given the chance to see a greater variety of work. The teacher responsible for the room might be invited to say a few words about the work on show to the governors before their meeting starts. Governors will also want to attend school functions such as plays and concerts but, whilst these events give some very valuable perspectives on school life, they are different from the normal classroom activities. One is aware of the difficulties that visiting during the day can present for some governors, particularly those in full-time employment. There is, however, no substitute for this sort of experience and every governor should, as a very minimum, try to visit the school when it is in session once a year. Governors who have had no contact with education since they themselves were at school need to remember that things have changed in education, as in everything else, and should not be surprised if they no longer find the children sitting at desks in neat rows with the teacher at the front wearing mortar-board and gown!

Governors' visits to the classroom

Governors are sometimes apprehensive before their first visit to a classroom and unsure of how to behave. Teachers may also be nervous, particularly if they are unused to having other adults in their classrooms while they are teaching and are uncertain about the purpose of the governor's visit. Governors find it helpful if they receive a specific invitation, 'Come and see my class next Tuesday afternoon', rather than the general suggestion 'Call in any time you are passing.' It is very difficult to take up such vague invitations. Teacher-governors have an important part to play here in introducing governors to teachers and in facilitating the governor's first visit which might even be to their own class. If at all possible the governor should try to meet the teacher beforehand to discuss the visit. The teacher can explain what will be happening and perhaps suggest one or two points in particular which the governor might look out for. The governor might be able to become involved during the lesson, perhaps by working with a small group of children or an individual. Both teacher and governor should behave as naturally as possible during the visit and the governor should endeavour to speak to the teacher afterwards, even if only to say 'thank you'. Governors should always look out for the positive and be ready to give praise where praise is due.

Some points for governors to look at when visiting a classroom are:

- How many children are there in the class? Is it a very large, or very small, group?
- How is the room arranged? Is the arrangement, and the room itself, suitable for the activity being undertaken?
- Are there displays around the room? Are the displays attractive and interesting and do they include pupils' work?
- What resources are being used and are there enough of them?
- How are the pupils grouped? Are they grouped by gender, by ability or in friendship groups?
- What are the children actually doing? Are they all undertaking the same task or is there differentiation by ability?
- How are the needs of those children with special educational needs being met?
- How are the children behaving? Are they interested and enthusiastic or listless and bored? How do they react to the governor as another adult?

Both governors and teachers may find it helpful if some guidelines are drawn up to help them in arranging the governors' visits.

TASK 3.5 ESTABLISHING GUIDELINES FOR GOVERNORS' VISITS TO SCHOOL
This Task could be very usefully undertaken by a small group of governors and teachers on behalf of their colleagues.

Bearing in mind the points which have been made in the chapter, draw up a set of written guidelines for both governors and teachers which will make governors' visits to classrooms more effective in your school. Distribute copies of the guidelines to all governors and teachers.

TASK 3.6 UNDERTAKING A CLASSROOM VISIT

This is a Task for individual governors, particularly those who have not previously undertaken a classroom visit.

Arrange to visit a teacher in his or her classroom, aiming to spend up to an hour with the class. If you are not specifically linked with a teacher and don't feel that you can approach one of the teachers yourself, ask the teacher-governor to introduce you to a teacher who would be happy to have you in his/her classroom. If there are guidelines on governors' visits to classrooms, refer to those. Try to spend time with the teacher before the lesson, discussing what the teacher will be trying to achieve and deciding what will be the focus for your observation. Explore and resolve any concerns which either of you has about the visit. After the visit discuss what you have seen and learned with the teacher.

CHAPTER 4

Managing the Work of the Governing Body

Our governors' meetings are not an effective forum for discussion.
(Secondary school governor)

In order to be effective governing bodies need to manage their work efficiently which means using their resources, especially time, to maximum effect. Governors will have many demands upon their time and they must be sure that the time which they are devoting to school business is used wisely. Much of the business of the governing body is conducted in meetings and therefore these need to be as well run as possible. Given their wide-ranging responsibilities, many governing bodies now seek to delegate some of their work to sub-groups and it is important that any such sub-groups with executive powers are legally constituted and that they have clear terms of reference. Governors should devote an appropriate proportion of their time to seeing the school 'in action' in order to foster the governor–staff partnership but also to see the curriculum in action.

Getting the most out of meetings

In order to be effective the governing body needs to be efficient; that is, it needs to use its resources in terms of governors' time and energy to maximum effect. Meetings of the governing body need to be well run if the school is to gain the maximum benefit and this has a number of implications for all governors. Where governors' meetings are held only once a term it may be difficult for governors to have a sense of continuous involvement in the life and work of the school. This situation is made worse if a governor happens to miss a termly meeting. The agenda for the meeting may also be a hindrance to governors' discussions of the work of the school, particularly where the agenda is over-long and fails to allow for discussion of the important issues affecting the school. Many governing bodies now meet twice a term in order to be able to deal adequately with their business, and this is certainly preferable to having just one meeting which drags on for three or four hours. Where the governing body does decide to have two meetings a term, both should have written agendas and minutes.

The effective conduct of meetings

The main factors which make for effective meetings are:

- A clear purpose for the meeting
- Good planning and preparation
- Comfortable surroundings
- Good chairmanship
- Good contributions from those attending
- Clear outcomes
- Reasonable length

In order to have a successful meeting there must be a well-planned agenda (with well-written supporting papers if necessary), well-prepared and self-disciplined members of the group and good chairmanship. Having an agenda which contributes towards the real work of the governing body is helped enormously if the governing body is clear about its purpose and priorities. The agenda should reflect those priorities so that matters which are seen as central to the school come early in the meeting and less important matters appear later. Chairs and headteachers need to give very careful consideration to the construction of the agenda for their meetings so that adequate time is allowed for discussion of key issues and the time is not wasted in the discussion of relatively unimportant matters. Good agendas make clear on which items decisions are required and where a report is either for discussion or to be noted without taking a decision.

The agenda and papers ought to reach the governors at least seven days in advance of the meeting so that they have the chance to study them properly beforehand. Unless absolutely unavoidable, long and complex papers should never be produced at the meeting itself. Where the agenda is drawn up by the LEA, rather than by the governors themselves, care needs to be taken to ensure that the agenda provided is not too long and that it acts as a stimulus to discussion rather than a strait-jacket. All governors need to be aware of the proper procedure for putting items on the agenda and 'Any other business' should be restricted to any item of real urgency which could not have been put on the agenda in advance. This agenda item should not be used as an opportunity for governors to air their pet grievances and there should certainly be no attempts to 'ambush' the headteacher. When a governor wishes to raise an issue, whether under 'Any other business' or not, the Chair and headteacher should be informed in advance as a matter of routine courtesy.

The meeting can be helped enormously if thought has been given beforehand to the time to be allotted to each of the items on the agenda, and this will often be a job for the Chair and the headteacher working together. An outline timetable can be put to the meeting at the start and any amendments made as suggested by other governors. It is not necessary to adhere slavishly to the timetable but it is surprising how having a time limit, however tentative, does tend to concentrate people's thoughts. Meetings which last much over two hours without a break tend to become counter-productive. People become tired, their attention wanders and some may have to leave for other commitments. If there is so much business on the agenda that the meeting cannot be completed in a reasonable length of time, it is probably better to hold two meetings or, alternatively, to pass some of the items to one or more sub-groups for consideration.

Sometimes people come out of a meeting which has not gone well blaming the Chair. This is often unfair because the success or otherwise of a meeting depends upon the effort of all the participants and not only upon the effectiveness of the Chair. A group of people who are acting as an effective team can often function perfectly well in discussion without a designated chair or group leader. Every governor should make it his or her business to be punctual and to come prepared to the meeting, having studied the agenda and any supporting papers beforehand. Governors need to discipline themselves to keep their own contributions brief, non-partisan and to the point, while at the same time being ready to listen tolerantly to the views of others and to accept and build upon their ideas. The way the furniture is arranged can have a surprising effect upon the atmosphere in which the meeting is conducted. The room should be well ventilated and governors need to be seated comfortably and not too far apart. A table or tables on which governors can put their papers can be helpful but should not be allowed to render the meeting unduly formal. A flip-chart can be a useful aid to stimulating ideas and in helping to keep track of the discussion. Refreshments may be served before the meeting or in the middle, in which case this can offer a useful break in the meeting and an opportunity for less formal discussion.

A good Chair will have ensured that the papers were distributed in good time and that the room and furniture are suitably arranged. He or she will seek to ensure that all governors are able to contribute and that all contributions are equally valued and to the point. The long-winded, pompous, repetitious and self-serving must not be allowed to dominate the meeting. Of course in a self-disciplined governing body working as an effective team these types will not exist! The Chair should ensure that the agenda is adhered to and also keep an eye on the clock. Once the Chair feels that everyone has had an opportunity to contribute to the discussion on a particular item, he or she should summarise and clarify the point which has been reached in the discussion. It may be that a formal proposition is required or the group may be satisfied that consensus has been reached. After any final contributions from governors the Chair should make sure that the Clerk to the governing body has minuted the views and/or decision of the governors correctly and clearly.

Good decision making

Good decisions are those which

- address the real problem;
- are made after consultation with those involved;
- are made on the basis of knowledge of all the facts;
- are made after a range of options has been considered;
- are communicated to those who have to put the decision into effect;
- have their effect and outcomes monitored.

When making decisions the governors should be certain that they are addressing the real problem, be clear about what the decision is intended to achieve and make sure that they have all the necessary information. In making major decisions the governors will wish to ensure that there has been adequate consultation with those involved in the outcomes of the decision. Governors should be aware of any constraints, for instance limits on spending, which exist. Often there will be a number of options for them to examine and they will consider the likely consequences of each very carefully. Once the decision has been made it must be communicated to all those who have to act upon it. Finally, there should be arrangements for the results of the decision to be monitored in order to see whether or not the desired outcome has been achieved or whether further changes are necessary.

> **TASK 4.1 HOW EFFECTIVE AND EFFICIENT ARE OUR MEETINGS?**
> *This is a short Task probably best undertaken by the whole governing body either before or after a full governors' meeting. This is a Task which requires honesty!*
>
> Are the meetings of your governing body as effective and as efficient as they could be? Is the agenda of a reasonable length, are the items in the right order and does it reflect the priorities of your school? Are supporting papers easy to understand? Are the agenda and any supporting papers distributed in good time? Do all governors come properly prepared to the meeting and is everyone who wishes to do so able to contribute fully?

The headteacher's report to the governors

The headteacher plays a crucial role when deciding which issues he or she will put before the governing body for discussion. The Education Act (No 2) 1986 gives governors the right to request a written report from the headteacher on any topic they choose. Normal practice is for headteachers to prepare a report for the termly meeting of their governing body. This report will be a key factor in determining the nature of the partnership between head and governors and will be a vital source of information about the school for the governors. It provides an opportunity for the head to communicate directly to every member of the governing body, and the style and tone of the report will do much to establish the way in which the head wishes to work with the governors.

The headteacher's report will be one of the most important items to be discussed at the governors' meeting and should certainly be placed high on the agenda. It may be helpful for newly appointed headteachers to discuss with their governors how best to present their reports so that the document is as helpful as possible to the governors in carrying out their work. There may be some topics which appear every term in the report such as the number of pupils on roll, while others will appear less frequently. It is important to ensure, however, that over a period of three or four terms every major area of the work of the school is covered.

A typical headteacher's report might include, in no particular order of priority, items on:

• The staff (appointments, changes in role, impending departures, etc.)

- The pupils (numbers actual and projected, successes, discipline, special needs, etc.)
- The curriculum (aims, policy statements, new developments, etc.)
- Parents (events for parents, the PTA, etc.)
- Resources (the budget, buildings and grounds, equipment, etc.)
- Liaison activities (links with other schools and agencies, pupil visits, community links, etc.).

The headteacher's report should enable the governing body to fulfil its proper functions by providing the governors with information about all aspects of the work of the school. The report should be written so that governors are clear about the purpose of each section – whether it is to inform, whether governors are being asked for their views or whether a decision is required. The report provides the headteacher with an excellent opportunity to ascertain the views of the governing body on matters of policy and to invite the governors to become involved in the decision-making process. The style in which the report is written is important; while it is a formal document, it should not be pompous or jargon-ridden but readable and accessible both in language and layout. Numbered sub-headings should be used to help break up the report into sections and where large amounts of statistical information have to be conveyed – for example examination and/or test results – these are probably best placed in an appendix. There is no reason why every word should have been written by the headteacher. It can provide variety of style and enhance communication between staff and governors if on occasion different teachers are asked to provide short reports on their work for the governors. The teacher could be invited to the governors' meeting to speak to his or her section of the report.

Delegation

Delegation is the giving of a task for which you still retain the ultimate responsibility to someone else with that person's agreement.

The governing body may choose to delegate some but not all of its functions to individuals or to groups. One of the greatest changes in the working practices of governing bodies brought about by the 1986 and subsequent Education Acts has been the setting up by the majority of governing bodies of standing sub-groups to deal with matters such as finance. Previously governors worked only in *ad hoc* sub-groups of the governing body on matters such as appointments or, more rarely, on disciplinary and complaints procedures. The proviso in the definition of delegation above about the agreement of the person to whom the job is delegated is an important one. It is no good delegating a job to someone who doesn't want it and who therefore won't carry it out properly!

It is important to stress once again that the day-to-day management of the school should be clearly in the hands of the headteacher and staff. Governors who attempt to interfere in such matters are usurping the proper authority of the teachers and will not foster the cause of partnership. Day-to-day management covers such matters as decisions about which teacher teaches which class, the discipline of pupils within the policy laid down by the governing body and the granting of short-term leave of absence to members of staff, again within the policy agreed by the governors.

Why Delegate?

Delegation helps to ensure

- Swifter and more appropriate decision making
- The transfer of routine matters, leaving freedom to concentrate on key issues
- Staff and governor development.

One can illustrate the virtues of delegation by a simple example. The governing body is responsible for deciding how the sum of money allocated to it for running the school is to be spent. However, for a governing body to attempt to concern itself in details such as the spending on pencils would be a recipe for disaster! The governors would have to meet every time a fresh supply of pencils was required and waste time deliberating over how many to purchase, of which type and from whom. The governing body therefore delegates to the headteacher decisions as to how precisely the sum of money allocated for educational supplies and services is to be spent. In all but the very smallest schools, it is likely that the headteacher will delegate still further. For instance, a sum of money might be allocated by the headteacher, doubtless after consultation, to be spent on the teaching of science. The teacher with overall responsibility for science teaching in the school will be responsible to the headteacher for the spending of that money. In a large secondary school there may be still further delegation to the teachers with responsibilities for teaching particular subjects within the overall science provision.

Delegation leads to swifter decision making and because the decisions are being made by those most closely involved in carrying them out, the decisions are more likely to be appropriate and effective. Delegation enables routine decisions and problems to be transferred downwards within the organisation, leaving those who have delegated them more scope to concentrate on broader issues and long-term planning. It is all too easy for the agendas of meetings at all levels to become so clogged with relatively trivial matters that the really important issues are never discussed. Finally, the delegation of decision making to junior members of staff is an important aspect of their professional development. The leader who attempts to do everything will not only fail to carry out his or her true leadership functions because of lack of time but will also deny more junior staff their rightful responsibilities.

Some responsibilities which governing bodies may **not** *delegate*

There are a number of important responsibilities which the governing body legally may not delegate, and some of these are set out below:

- The co-option and appointment of governors;
- Approval of the annual governors' report to parents;
- Ensuring that legal requirements on the admission of pupils are met (county and voluntary schools);
- The preparation of a curriculum statement;
- Ensuring that the legal requirements on religious education and collective worship are met;
- Approving the school's policy on sex education;
- Ensuring that there is a balanced treatment of political issues;
- Preparing a statement about pupil behaviour;
- Approval of the annual budget;
- Approval of a policy on charging for 'extras' and basis on which charges may be waived;
- Determining the times of school sessions and dates of school terms.

There are certain other key functions which should in any case not be delegated, regardless of the legal requirements. A wise governing body will not delegate the final approval of overall objectives and policies, although it may be sensible for the preparatory work to be undertaken by a sub-group. It should be clear from what has been said about the importance of shared aims and values (see chapter 2 on Building the Team) that the final ratification of a policy must be in the hands of the group as a whole and be seen as a shared responsibility. Communication between the members of the governing body must involve everyone and team-building activities must also by their very nature include everyone. Any situation which leads to a small group being 'in the know' to the exclusion of others – except on matters which require confidentiality – will destroy team spirit. Finally, monitoring overall progress towards the achievement of key objectives is probably too important a matter to be left to a small group and ought to remain a responsibility of the governing body as whole.

Committees or working parties?

The governing body can, if it so wishes, delegate some of its functions to working parties or to committees. There are significant differences between these two types of organisation as related to school governing bodies. A committee may be given delegated power to act, while a working party may only make recommendations with final approval resting with the governing body as a whole. Non-governors may be co-opted onto both committees and working parties and there are often advantages in doing this. Any such co-optees have no vote in a committee. Because a committee has delegated power, it may only be set up by a majority vote at a meeting of the full governing body at which at least two-thirds of the governors are present. A committee must follow the same procedural rules as the governing body itself in terms of the appointment of a Chair and Vice-Chair, and the publication of agenda and minutes. Decisions made by committees which have failed to follow the rules have been successfully challenged on procedural grounds, rather than over the correctness or otherwise of the decision.

The characteristics of committees and working parties are contrasted below:

	Committees	Working Parties
Decision-making powers	Yes	No
Formal agenda and minutes required	Yes	Not a legal requirement, but useful, nonetheless
Need to report back to the full governing body	Yes	Yes
Quorum needed to set up	2/3 of governors	1/3 of governors
Non-governor members	Yes (may not vote)	Yes
Limitations on size	Sometimes	No

Because of the restrictions on the setting up and operation of committees, many governing bodies have chosen to set up working parties instead. Every governing body will, however, require a properly constituted committee to deal with disciplinary and complaints procedures relating to members of staff. The governing body as a whole cannot deal with these matters. This is because, in the event of an appeal, natural justice requires that there is a group of governors who were not involved in the original decision available to hear that appeal. Similarly, the operation of a staff pay policy which has been agreed by the governing body as a whole should be in the hands of a committee so that, once again, any appeal against a decision of that committee can be heard by a fresh group of governors. Whether or not teacher-governors should serve on these committees is a matter for individual governing bodies and teacher-governors to decide. Teacher-governors are not barred from membership of any sub-group just because they are teachers. They operate under the same restrictions as any other governor – that is, they must withdraw from any discussion in which their personal interest is greater than that of any other member of the group. Teacher-governors may sit on appointment panels if they and the other governors so wish. However, a teacher who was the third member of a department could not be involved in the appointment of the head of that department if the second teacher in the department was a candidate for the post. In such a case the teacher-governor has an interest because he or she might gain promotion if the number two gained the head of department post.

A governing body which is operating as an effective team will be sure of its shared purpose and common aspirations and will therefore be ready to delegate to colleagues. There is no point in delegating to a group if their discussion is simply to be repeated in the subsequent meeting of the full governing body. There should be precise terms of reference so that the sub-group is quite clear about what it is being asked to do on behalf of the governing body, and a mechanism by which the sub-group reports back to the governing body. Remember, too, that while the governing body may delegate the task, the ultimate responsibility remains with the governing body.

TASK 4.2 REVIEWING YOUR DELEGATION ARRANGEMENTS

This Task could be undertaken by the governing body as a whole or by a sub-group which will report back to the full governing body.

Review the delegation arrangements at present operated by your governing body. Is everyone clear precisely what has been delegated? Are there clear terms of reference and are the arrangements for reporting back equally clear? Are any committees which have been set up legally constituted? Is there scope for further delegation?

Governors and the curriculum

Finance and the curriculum are the two things that make the school tick and I don't think that you can be effective [as a governor] unless you really know something about them.

(Secondary school governor)

The curriculum is the range of learning opportunities which the school provides for its pupils. This includes the formal lessons in classroom, laboratory, gymnasium or on the sports field. It also includes those activities arranged by the school which take place outside the normal school hours, such as dramatic and musical productions, matches against teams from other schools and school trips and visits. There is also what is termed the 'hidden curriculum'. This is the set of attitudes and values which pupils acquire, often sub-consciously, through being members of the school. This hidden curriculum depends heavily upon the ethos of the school and the relationship between the adults (including the governors) and the pupils.

Prior to 1988, schools had considerable freedom in decisions about the curriculum which they could offer. The 1944 Education Act had made Religious Education compulsory in all state schools, but there was no *legal* requirement to teach any other subject, not even English or Maths! This freedom could produce some unfortunate effects with some children making early choices about the subjects they were to pursue which might limit their later choice of career. It was also difficult for children who moved and had to change schools, particularly towards the end of their time in school. The 1988 Educational Reform Act established a National Curriculum which all children in state schools (but not the independent sector) must follow and this consists of three core subjects (English, Maths and Science) together with seven Foundation subjects. These are Art, Geography, History, Modern Languages (for 11 to 16 year olds only), Music, Physical Education and Technology. Welsh is an additional core subject in the Principality. Pupils are still required to study Religious Education alongside the National Curriculum subjects. In addition to laying down the subjects which children were to study the Act also set out a scheme for testing all children at ages 7, 11, 14 and 16 via Standard Assessment Tasks (SATs).

Critics complained that the amount of content in such a curriculum overloaded pupils and provided no flexibility for them to pursue their special interests and abilities. Some subjects which had traditionally appeared on the timetable did not appear in the National Curriculum and might therefore be squeezed out altogether. There was considerable opposition to the initial proposals on testing which were seen as unduly burdensome and bureaucratic. Since its introduction, there has been significant modification to the National Curriculum and to its associated testing arrangements, particularly following the review led by Sir Ron Dearing in 1993. It has been proposed that there should be no further changes for at least five years in order to provide a period of stability so that the new curriculum can be fully implemented.

The governors must establish their own aims for the curriculum of the school. This is certainly a task which they will wish to undertake in close partnership with the headteacher and staff – indeed the governors are legally obliged to consult the headteacher on this issue. The governors must consider the LEA's statement on the curriculum, and while the school's curriculum may reflect the specific needs of the school, it must meet the requirements of the National Curriculum and provide for Religious Education. It is for the governing body to consider and determine, having consulted the headteacher, the question of whether sex education should form part of the curriculum of the school. The governors must make a written statement of their policy on sex education with regard to its content and organisation.

The traditional view of a teacher is of someone standing at the front of a class, with children sitting in neat rows at their desks. The governor who visits the school regularly will soon come to realise that a wide range of approaches is in current use in order to promote pupil learning. Children learn best in a variety of ways and therefore teachers need to use a variety of different methods. Sometimes the children will be working silently on their own, sometimes they will be working in small groups and sometimes the teacher will be speaking to the whole class. Whatever style is being used, it is vital that the teacher has high expectations of each and every child.

Since children progress at different rates, this may mean that children in the same class are not all working on the same task at the same time. This provision of different tasks according to the differing abilities of the children is called 'differentiation', an approach calling for considerable organisational skills on the part of the teacher. Some children within a class may have been identified as having special educational needs (SEN). These needs may be short- or long-term and may be due to emotional, physical or mental handicaps. Special provision has to be made for such children, for example, adaptations of the building to provide for children in wheelchairs, or the employment of classroom assistants to help children with learning difficulties. The 1993 Education Act sets out a framework within which governors are required to make provision for children with special educational needs in their school.

Governing bodies must:

- Do their best to secure that the necessary provision is made for any pupil with special educational needs;
- Identify a 'responsible person', and ensure that, when that person has been informed by the LEA that a pupil has special educational needs, those needs are made known to all who are likely to teach that child;
- Ensure that teachers in the school are aware of the importance of identifying, and providing for, those pupils who have special educational needs;
- Consult with the LEA, Funding Agency where appropriate, and governing bodies of other schools where necessary;
- Ensure that any pupil with special educational needs joins in the activities of the school with other pupils as far as possible;
- Report annually to parents on their policy for pupils with special educational needs.

(For further details see Circular 6/94, 'The Organisation of Special Educational Provision', published by the DFE).

The governing body should, therefore, in consultation with the headteacher, decide on a special needs policy and there must be appropriate funding and staffing provision for the children concerned. The named 'responsible person' will often be the headteacher or, in larger schools, the teacher with responsibility for working with children with special educational needs, but could be a governor. The governing body might, if they so wished, set up a committee to monitor special needs provision in the school or, alternatively, designate one governor who will have oversight of this important area of the school's work.

TASK 4.3 FINDING OUT ABOUT THE CURRICULUM
This is a Task for individual governors, especially newly appointed ones.

Ask a teacher (perhaps the teacher whose class you visited) to explain to you the broad outline of the curriculum of the school. Ask about recent developments and forthcoming changes. How is the curriculum resourced? What provision is made for children with special educational needs?

TASK 4.4 REVIEWING THE GOVERNORS' CURRICULUM POLICIES

This Task might be undertaken by the whole governing body or by a smaller group – the curriculum sub-group if there is one.

Review the curriculum policies which have been laid down by the governing body. These could include policies on religious education, sex education and special needs provision, as well as any more general statement on the curriculum.

CHAPTER 5

Governors and the Effective School

> The effective school is one that achieves more than could be expected on the basis of its intake.
>
> (Effective Schools Project, Australia 1991–93)

> An effective school is one which brings children from lower income families to the same level of competence as successful children from middle income families.
>
> (Connecticut School Effectiveness Programme, 1978–88)

In this chapter we shall seek to explore the central issue of school effectiveness and how governing bodies may contribute to school improvement. Pupils at some schools perform better than those at others and HM Chief Inspector has recently gone so far as to identify publicly schools whose performance has improved significantly. Under the Grants for Education Support and Training (GEST) scheme for 1995–6 there is a category identified as 'School Effectiveness' and this includes funds for school management training as well as for the support and training of governors. Governors and staff together will wish to do all that they can to identify any weaknesses in their schools and to bring about improvement. Improvement comes through effective development planning and the chapter includes some advice on the planning process and suggestions as to ways in which governors might become involved. As indicated in chapter 1, an important aspect of the role of the governing body is working with the staff in continually monitoring the work of the school, though it must be recognised that this process does take time.

What *is* an effective school? By what criteria should the effectiveness of schools be judged? What evidence should be gathered in order to be able to judge the effectiveness of a school? How can schools be made more effective? These are vital questions for anyone who has the best interests of children and young people at heart, whether they be governors, parents, teachers or members of the general public. The debate about educational standards has been going on for many years – in the

United Kingdom most energetically since Prime Minister Jim Callaghan's famous speech at Ruskin College in 1976, in which he raised the issue of the performance of the country's schools. Discussion is still going on, but since 1993, for the first time, there is a system by which the work of all schools is to be regularly reviewed, *to a published set of criteria*, by inspectors appointed by the Office for Standards in Education (OFSTED). The point about publishing the criteria is not insignificant. Schools had been inspected for many years by Her Majesty's Inspectors (HMI), although not so frequently or as regularly as they will be under the new system. Previously, however, schools never knew by what criteria they were being judged, what precisely the inspectors were looking for, or what standards were expected. Whether or not the governors and staff agree or disagree with all the criteria, at least they now know the basis upon which their work will be assessed.

TASK 5.1 WHAT DO WE MEAN BY AN EFFECTIVE SCHOOL?

This Task may be undertaken by individual governors or teachers but is probably best done by governors and teachers working together in pairs, fours or groups of eight. If the group is a very large one, the outcomes from the smaller groups should be compared and discussed at the end of the activity.

List ten criteria by which you would wish the quality of the education provided in your school to be judged. You can if you wish prioritise them but this is not essential.

One might expect that the criteria which the group or individual has established bear some relation to the published aims of the school. After all, it is this set of aims which the governors, parents and staff together have decided upon as reflecting their priorities for the school. One would therefore expect these aims to be closely linked to the criteria by which the quality of the education provided by the school is to be judged. When Task 5.1 has been completed, the list of criteria from the OFSTED *Framework for Inspection* which is printed below should be considered and compared with the list of criteria produced by the group. This will almost certainly provoke further discussion and possibly some amendment of the original list. Amongst the points which might be considered are the following:

● The OFSTED list is divided into key issues and contributory factors.

Does this seem a sensible division to you and do you agree with the placing of each of the criteria?

- Notice the high priority which OFSTED attaches to pupils' learning and attainment. Do these criteria figure in your list and where have you placed them?
- You might have something in your list about pupils feeling happy and secure at school. Where do criteria of this nature figure in the OFSTED list?
- Efficiency of management is seen as a key issue by the OFSTED inspectors. What does efficiency mean in terms of the management of a school and does it have a place in your list?
- Note the emphasis placed by the OFSTED Framework on the spiritual, moral, social and cultural development of the pupils. Where does such development feature in your criteria?
- Equality of opportunity is stressed in the OFSTED list. Does your school have a policy on equal opportunities and, more significantly, how well does it work in practice?
- Did your group identify 'assessment, recording and reporting' as one of the criteria? If not, why not?

Probably other issues will arise in the discussion.

OFSTED criteria

The criteria used by OFSTED inspectors in making their judgements about schools are as follows:

The overall judgement about the school should be based on the inspection team's evaluation of:

- the standards of achievement:
- the quality of education provided:
- the efficiency with which resources are managed:
- the spiritual, moral, social and cultural development of pupils.

The Framework for Inspection, p.17, (OFSTED, May 1994)

The main findings of the inspecting team will therefore be presented under the following headings:

Standards and Quality

- Standards of achievement
- Quality of learning

The efficiency of the school

Pupils' personal development and behaviour

- Pupil's spiritual, moral, social and cultural development
- Behaviour and discipline
- Attendance

Subjects of the curriculum and other curricular provision

The factors which are seen by OFSTED as contributing to these central themes are:

- Quality of teaching
- Assessment, recording and reporting
- Quality and range of the curriculum
- Equality of opportunity
- Provision for pupils with special educational needs
- Management and administration
- Staff, learning resources and accommodation
- Pupil's welfare and guidance
- Links with parents, agencies and other institutions.

Parental views on the criteria for effectiveness might well be sought at the annual parents meeting with governors; it would make an interesting debate. However it is arrived at, once the list of criteria has been established, the next question must be: how far is the school achieving these standards of effectiveness? In order to answer that question, governors and staff together need to move on to consideration of what evidence is required to show that the school is meeting each of the criteria and where such evidence might be found. Suppose, for instance, that in the list of criteria of effectiveness there is one relating to pupil behaviour. What sort of evidence would one wish to gather about pupil behaviour in the school and where might one find it? One might ask the teachers for their professional judgement as to how the pupils behave in and out of the classroom, and one could ask the parents and other adults connected with the school for their views. One could study records of truancy and exclusion rates and almost certainly one would wish to observe the pupils themselves, both in and out of the classroom. Evidence from all these sources would be brought together in arriving at a judgement about the behaviour of the pupils in the school.

TASK 5.2 HOW CAN WE FIND OUT WHETHER OUR SCHOOL IS EFFECTIVE?

This activity is probably best undertaken by governor–teacher pairs. It will probably take up to 30 minutes per criterion at first, but if the pair undertakes a second or third criterion, less time will usually be required for successive criteria.

For each of the criteria in your agreed list draw up a table of the evidence you would seek in order to establish the extent to which that criterion was being met and note where that evidence would be found.

Possible sources include professional judgements by individuals and/or groups, views and opinions, pupils work, records of attainment and/or test/exam results, observation of pupils and routinely collected statistics such as those from attendance registers.

Eventually there should be a set of statements about what evidence would be sought and where it would be found for each of the criteria of effectiveness. If necessary, each governor–teacher pair could be asked to consider more than one criterion in order to complete the task or alternatively the task could be spread over more than one session. One potential difficulty which may begin to emerge from the discussions is the time needed to collect the information. Remember that much of the information may already be available in one form or another. Perhaps governors and teachers have already established the sort of *rapport* through which governors could be involved in the data collection process. Governors are a valuable resource for the school and some or all of them may be able to spare some time to help. As indicated in chapter 3, governors' visits to school are likely to be much more effective if they have a specific focus, and the sort of information-gathering exercise which is being suggested will provide an admirable purpose for these visits. Governors and teachers will be enabled to engage together in a meaningful discussion about educational issues. Governors and staff should not try to start everywhere at once but begin by looking for data on just one or two of the criteria, perhaps choosing areas which have already emerged as priorities for improvement.

TASK 5.3 COLLECTING THE EVIDENCE

This Task can be undertaken by governors alone, teachers alone or by governors and teachers together. The time taken will depend to a large extent upon the data to be collected.

Collect the data by whatever means you have decided upon in order to obtain the evidence you need to satisfy yourselves that your school is meeting the agreed criteria of effectiveness.

The data collection will of course take some time – perhaps several weeks for each of the criteria – but once all the data on a particular criterion has been collected, the governors and staff can begin their discussion as to how far the school is going towards meeting the various criteria which they decided upon for themselves as their measures of effectiveness.

TASK 5.4 WHERE CAN WE DO BETTER?

At a joint governor–staff meeting explore together the implications of your findings.

Where is the school meeting its objectives and where is further development required? Are these areas for improvement already noted in the School Development Plan or do they need to be added? If they are to be included will something else have to go? Remember that if everything is a priority, then nothing is! Would you be able to justify your list of priorities to an outsider?

What makes an effective school?

Children were more likely to show good behaviour and good scholastic attainments if they attended some schools than if they attended others.

(*Fifteen Thousand Hours*, Rutter *et al.*,1979, London: Open Books)

There is clear evidence from research in the United Kingdom and around the world that some schools are more effective than others in apparently very similar circumstances. What are the factors accounting for these differences? Below are two lists of characteristics of effective schools drawn from two different sources. Governors and staff should study them carefully and honestly try to identify those characteristics which they believe are present in their own school and those which are currently absent or deficient.

1. According to Reid, Hopkins and Holly (*Towards the Effective School*, Blackwell, 1987), research indicates that effective schools display the following characteristics:

- There is good leadership from the head and senior staff;
- The school is well managed;
- There is a positive ethos in the school;
- The school is orderly at all times;
- The teaching is of high quality;
- Teaching is seen as the most important activity;
- The curriculum is as important for low-achieving pupils as for high achievers;
- Pupils receive regular feedback on their performance;
- Pupils expect and receive high professional standards from their teachers;
- Proper use is made of classroom teaching time;
- Reading, writing and mathematics are emphasised;
- Pupils are encouraged to participate in the running of the school;
- The buildings are clean and well cared for.

2. A report by the School Management Task Force, (*Developing School Management: the way forward*, HMSO, 1990) says that effective schools may be seen to have the following characteristics:

- Good leadership offering breadth of vision and the ability to motivate others;
- Appropriate delegation with involvement in policy-making by staff other than the head;
- Clearly established and purposeful staffing structures;
- Well qualified staff with an appropriate blend of experience and expertise;
- Clear aims and associated objectives applied with care and consistency;
- Effective communications and clear systems of record-keeping and assessment;
- The means to identify and develop pupils' particular strengths, promoting high expectations by both teachers and pupils;
- A coherent curriculum which considers pupils' experience as a whole and demonstrates concern for their development within society;
- A positive ethos: an orderly yet relaxed atmosphere of work;
- A suitable working environment;
- Skills of deploying and managing material resources;
- Good relationships with parents, the local community and sources of external support;

• The capacity to manage change, to solve problems and to develop organically.

Note that the characteristics of effective schools given in the two lists refer to different aspects of the work of the school. Some, such as the emphasis on the use of time in the classroom or record-keeping and assessment, are very much concerned with teaching practice in the classroom. A second group of characteristics is more to do with the way in which the school is managed – for instance, appropriate delegation arrangements or the provision of a suitable working environment. A third, very important group refers to the ethos of the school. The presence of a positive ethos is mentioned in both lists and there are other associated issues such as relationships with parents. A governing body, working in partnership with the staff, will be active in addressing particularly the characteristics which refer to the management and ethos of the school.

TASK 5.5 HOW WELL ARE THE FACTORS LEADING TO SCHOOL EFFECTIVENESS DEVELOPED IN OUR SCHOOL?
This Task will probably take an hour or more and might be delegated to a small group of governors and teachers who could then report back to the governing body and the staff.

Consider carefully the factors leading to school effectiveness which are identified in the two lists above. Are there any factors which can be identified as requiring enhancement in your school? Prioritise these and consider their place in the School Development Plan.

School effectiveness: the governor's role

Some ways in which the governing body can contribute towards the effectiveness of its school are:

• Work in partnership with the staff;
• Help towards the establishment of a climate for school improvement;
• Work with the staff to prepare a good development plan;
• Appoint staff, especially senior staff, who are committed to school improvement;
• Work with the staff to monitor and evaluate progress;
• Set an example by seeking to improve the performance of the governing body (see chapter 6).

While governors may make a considerable contribution towards making their school more effective, they are unable to do it on their own. The headteacher and staff, as the professionals working daily in the school, must have the most significant input. Where governors and staff can work in the sort of partnership which has been described, the contribution of both groups is likely to be most effective. The governors will play their part by ensuring that the aims of the school are clear, agreed to and understood by all concerned. The governing body and senior staff will provide leadership by sharing a sense of purpose and a common vision. That vision for the school needs to be clearly articulated and made known to all involved. Governors will demonstrate their faith in the staff and pupils, and through the appointment of suitable staff will ensure that the school is well led. Through their involvement in the development planning process, governors will ensure that the priorities for improvement are clear, that adequate resources have been deployed to meet those priorities and that there are clear targets to be achieved. Governors can work alongside the staff in the all-important task of monitoring and evaluation.

A positive climate for school improvement

There is strong evidence to suggest that establishing a climate of school improvement is an essential prerequisite of successful innovation, and the governing body has an important part to play in establishing a climate in which improvement can take place. Working in partnership with the staff and by encouragement and support, governors can do much to establish an atmosphere in which it is possible to admit that there are things in the school capable of improvement. Governors and staff together will share a determination that areas of the school *shall* improve.

It is most likely that a positive climate for school improvement will occur when

- Governors and staff place a premium on staff and governor development;
- Governors, staff, parents and pupils all have a voice in decision making;
- Governors and staff make time to reflect upon progress;
- Governors and senior staff provide leadership;
- Governors and staff plan together.

When considering the annual budget for the school, governors should ensure that appropriate funding is allocated to the provision of in-service training (INSET) for the staff and themselves. This allocation will naturally be linked to the priorities which have been established in the School Development Plan. Thus, if Special Needs is a priority area, appropriate training for one or more members of staff, and possibly a governor, may be envisaged. The needs of individuals have to be carefully balanced against and aligned with the needs of the school as a whole.

The need for management development and training should not be overlooked and this should be funded from the INSET budget. The governors should resist the temptation to neglect their own training and development. Funds are currently provided within school budgets under the GEST arrangements for governor training and the money should be used for this purpose and not diverted towards staff training or other purposes. One can understand the wish of governors to see that the needs of the children and staff are fully met first, but to neglect their own training altogether is a short-sighted policy. There could be serious consequences if, for instance, governors were unaware of certain legal requirements because no member of the governing body attended training sessions.

Governors working in the ways described here will be involved in planning for the school's future and should be concerned to see that there is the maximum possible involvement by all concerned in the decision-making processes. It is sometimes felt that involving staff or parents in decision making is an abdication of power and responsibility. It is not being suggested that decisions are necessarily taken on the basis of 'one person one vote'. There is, however, strong evidence to suggest that when people have been genuinely consulted and have had an opportunity to put their point of view, they will accept and feel committed to the eventual decision, even when it is not their own preferred outcome. Governors and staff working in partnership will naturally wish to consult together and to bring parents and pupils into the consultation process as and when appropriate.

Evidence from schools which have shown real improvement suggests that thinking in a systematic manner about the way in which the school is progressing is helpful. This reflection depends on an on-going process of data-collection involving as many members of staff as possible. However, it is not sufficient merely to collect the data. The school needs to have a strategy through which that data is examined in order to review progress and to evaluate the effectiveness of changes which have been introduced. Governors can assist in this process by being involved in the data-collection and by inviting regular reports on progress towards the achievement of the priorities established in the School Development Plan. In this way governors are kept informed and will be much better placed to contribute to the planning process in the following year.

TASK 5.6 IMPROVING OUR SCHOOL

This Task could be undertaken by individual governors and/or members of staff, by a small group of governors and staff or by the whole governing body and/or staff.

Consider the factors necessary for school improvement which are set out above. How far are those factors present in the school and are there areas which need additional emphasis? Is in-service training required and, if so, how can it best be arranged?

School development planning

The purpose of development planning is to assist the school to introduce changes successfully, so that the quality of teaching and standards of learning are improved.

(Development planning: A Practical Guide, DES, 1991)

Schools and colleges exist in order to provide the best possible education for the children and young people in them. The aim of this book is to help governors and teachers to develop a shared vision for their school which will assist them towards school improvement. School improvement is about raising standards, enhancing quality and increasing efficiency, and is in the interests of all concerned – pupils, parents, governors and staff. Schools do not become more effective of their own accord. Achieving school improvement depends on the determination of the governors, headteacher and staff that the school will improve its performance through sound development planning. A well thought out and agreed School Development Plan is at the heart of the work of every effective school, so it is important that governors and teachers are clear about the purposes of the Plan.

TASK 5.7 WHY HAVE A SCHOOL DEVELOPMENT PLAN?
This activity could be undertaken by a group of governors, by a group of teachers, or ideally by a group of governors and teachers together.

Complete the following phrase:
'Our School Development Plan helps us to...'

Almost certainly the group will come up with a number of areas of the school's planning and management which are (or should be) assisted by the presence of a good Development Plan in the school.

A good Development Plan depends upon having a clear idea of the goal at which one wishes to arrive, an equally precise knowledge of the current situation and a clear and agreed set of steps by which the desired ends are to be achieved.

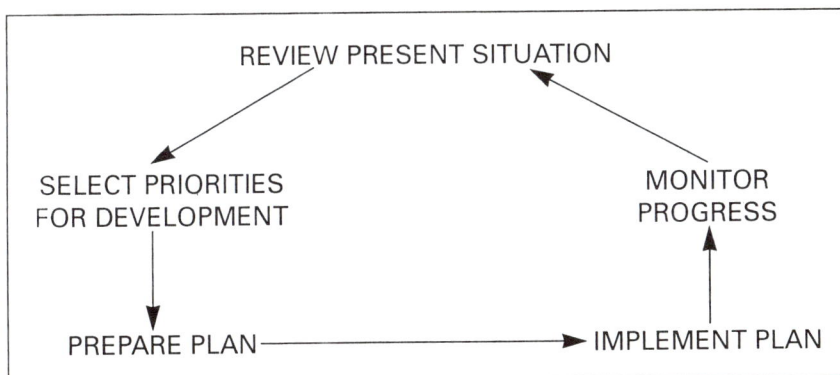

Figure 5.1: The School Development Planning Cycle

School development planning is, or should be, an ongoing cyclical process, moving from reviewing the present situation, through planning, implementation, monitoring and back again to review (see Figure 5.1). 'Success depends as much on the quality of the planning as on the specific content of the plan' (*Development Planning: A Practical Guide*, DES, 1991). Effective development planning starts with a review of the work of the school. Ideally this review or audit should be an ongoing process with information being collected throughout the school year, rather than in a rush just before the next plan is being prepared. Only by establishing clearly the present position in the school is it possible to plan properly how to arrive at the desired goal. It is possible to attempt a very wide-ranging review and there are published materials such as the *Guidelines for Review and Internal Development in Schools* (GRIDS, Schools Council, 1984, updated 1988) available to help in this process. However, the time and resources which such an enterprise requires should not be underestimated. Success may be more likely if governors and staff concentrate upon one small part of the work of the school at first, especially if this is an area which has already been recognised as in need of improvement. If success can be achieved in a relatively small scale improvement, this will provide encouragement for the future. Planned improvement should always be linked back to the fundamental aims of the school but must also take account of any financial constraints. If governors and staff have already undertaken Tasks 5.1, 5.2 and 5.3, this will have helped firstly in establishing where the governors and staff jointly wish the school to be and, secondly, in discovering something of where the school is now. To the perceptions of governors and staff may be added parental views, evidence from performance indicators such as examination results, and the views of OFSTED or LEA inspectors.

Once the current situation in the school has been established, governors and staff together will need to consider carefully which development priorities to set. In all schools at any time there will be areas of the school's work which are capable of development. In addition to areas for improvement which are identified by the staff and governors there will usually be other issues imposed or suggested by external agencies which require attention. Examples of externally imposed changes are the National Curriculum and teacher appraisal schemes. An OFSTED report on the school would almost certainly highlight areas for possible development. The long list of possibilities which emerges will almost certainly have to be shortened. The purpose of development planning is to identify where the priorities lie so that appropriate resources, whether of money, staff or time, can be allocated to them. Unless there is a clear identification of priorities it is possible that the resources will be spread so thinly across all areas that it becomes impossible for significant improvement to occur anywhere.

Listed below are a number of points to consider in drawing up the shortlist of priorities:

- Don't attempt too much. Better to do a few things well than fail across the board. Avoid 'innovation overload'.
- Try to choose ideas which can be linked together into a coherent framework rather than several disconnected projects.
- Consider the urgency/need/desirability of the alternatives.
- Consider the size and scope of the alternatives. Do some of the projects

require phasing because they are too big to be undertaken in one year?
● Ensure wide consultation at this stage.

The School Development Plan sets out the priorities for development looking ahead for two or three years with the priorities for the second and third years more tentatively outlined because circumstances may change. Once these priorities have been established, more detailed planning can begin.

The Action Plan

The Action Plan starts from the objective(s) specified in the overall Development Plan and helps to translate ideas into action. It has to be very specific since its purpose is to make clear to every governor and to every member of staff precisely what has to be achieved, by whom and by when. The Plan includes a statement of the resources to be allocated, details of how and when progress will be reviewed, and sets out very clearly what the targets are and how success is to be measured. Let us suppose, for instance, that one of the priorities in the School Development Plan is to improve pupil literacy. Under this heading the Action Plan might include as specific objectives increasing the number of times each child reads to an adult per week and increasing the number of books from the school library which each child reads in a term. The targets to be achieved might include a specified increase in average scores on a standard reading test over the year and a specified number of books to be borrowed by a child in a term. By setting clear goals in this way it will be possible, when the next review process comes round, to judge the success or otherwise of the initiative much more easily.

The characteristics of a good Action Plan are that it

● refers to the objective(s) set out in the Development Plan;
● includes specific targets and success criteria;
● makes clear exactly who is to do what;
● includes deadlines for the completion of tasks;
● includes arrangements for monitoring progress;
● includes details of the resources required to complete the task;
● includes details, with costs, of any necessary training required.

Once the Plan has been finalised, it must be put into operation through the staff who will have been fully involved in the planning process.

Reviewing implementation

The final stage is to review progress towards the achievement of the aims set out in the Plan, paving the way for the whole process to repeat itself. The evaluation of the extent to which the aims of the Plan have been achieved is an important stage and one which is all too easily overlooked. Largely because of the high rate of change imposed upon schools in the recent past teachers have tended to move on to the next initiative without properly evaluating the success of the last. By reviewing performance honestly there is an opportunity to build upon success and perhaps to avoid repeating failure. Building criteria for success into the Plan makes that review process much easier. It is, however, as important to review the *way* in which the success was achieved as it is to review the outcomes themselves. Schools need to develop a climate which can sustain continuous self-improvement and in which governors and staff feel confident of their own capabilities.

TASK 5.8 REVIEWING THE PLANNING PROCESS

The first part of this Task could be carried out by one or two individuals before the whole group of governors and/or teachers meets to undertake the main part of the Task. Copies of the chart or timetable could be distributed to all members of the group or a large chart could be put up where all can see it.

Part 1
Produce a flow-chart or timetable to show the process by which last year's School Development Plan was produced in your school.

Part 2
In the light of the outcome of Part 1, review the development planning process within your school.

Questions which might be asked include:

- Are planning and the management of change really integrated into the day-to-day life of the school?
- Is there an ethos of working together and a sense of partnership within the school?
- Do the planning and management systems within the school give direction and purpose?
- Was there adequate consultation? Were enough people invited to contribute ideas in the early stages? Was everyone involved clear about the way in which the plan was being developed?
- Did the process start soon enough or were the final stages too rushed?
- Was enough account taken of external influences during the planning process?

Governors' involvement in the planning process

Some ways in which governors might involve themselves in the essential review process have already been described. The extent to which some or all of the governors participate in drawing up the Plan itself will vary from school to school, depending on the particular circumstances. On the one hand, the governing body could leave it all to the headteacher and staff. At the other extreme, governors could attempt to share in the day-to-day operation of the Development Plan. Neither of these two extremes reflects the sort of partnership which we are seeking to develop. In the past, the involvement of governing bodies has sometimes been limited to giving a final seal of approval to a Development Plan which has been drawn up by the headteacher and staff. It is almost impossible for the governors to feel any sort of 'ownership' of the Plan in this situation, and to treat the governors in this way is to negate the spirit of governor–staff partnership for which schools should be striving.

One possible way of involving governors in the planning process is to invite them to attend a professional development day during which the staff will debate the Plan for the forthcoming year. Alternatively, a sub-group of the governing body might be set up specifically to work with the staff on the Plan or an individual governor, perhaps with some special expertise, might be involved. At the very least, governors could be invited to contribute to the preliminary drafting of the list of possible areas for development. Once a shortlist of priorities has been established, governors could be invited to comment on them before detailed Action Plans are drawn up by the staff. This would provide an opportunity to discuss any major resource implications which will need to be considered when drawing up the school's budget.

The governing body has an important part to play by asking questions about the school's progress towards the achievement of its goals. We have already discussed in detail how governors might be involved during the audit stage of the planning. Governors should ensure that the school honestly and regularly reviews its work and that all of the appropriate available evidence is taken into account. During the actual planning process governors will be concerned to ensure that both staff and governors are being properly involved and that it is clear what decisions are being made and by whom. During the implementation stage, the governing body should be kept informed of progress and told about any unexpected major difficulties which might require alterations to the original Plan, including the deployment of additional resources. Finally, as the cycle begins to repeat itself, the governors should be involved in the evaluation of the success of the plan as they begin the preparation of planning for the next year.

The following list is a summary of the ways in which the governing body might participate in the planning process:

- Governors have a part to play in setting the ethos of the school which should be one in which there is an atmosphere of partnership and a readiness to seeks ways of improving performance.
- Governors can work alongside the staff in the task of gathering the evidence in the review process.
- Governors may have experience of, and expertise in, planning gained in other organisations which they can share with the staff.
- Governors may work alongside the staff in the evaluation phase of the process, helping the staff to gather evidence as to the success of the innovations.
- Governors can ensure that time is spent on discussing educational issues at all their meetings.
- Governors see the development plan 'in action' through their visits to classrooms and/or their links with classes/teachers/subject areas.
- A 'Governors' Development Plan', which lists priorities for the governors in the coming year, could be included in the main Development Plan. This might include such items as:

  - Produce, in partnership with the staff, a new policy on special educational needs;
  - Review with the staff the operation of the school's equal opportunities policy;
  - Set up a working group to suggest ways of improving communication between governors and parents.

TASK 5.9 HOW COULD GOVERNORS CONTRIBUTE TO THE PLANNING PROCESS?

This Task could be undertaken by the whole governing body, together with the headteacher and senior staff, or by a smaller group of governors, together with the head and senior staff. It will take up to one hour.

Review the current pattern of involvement of governors in the school development planning process in the light of what you have read.

Can governors become more fully involved in order to reflect more closely the governor–teacher partnership in the school?

CHAPTER 6

How Effective is your Governing Body?

Governing bodies are, on occasion and for a variety of reasons, deflected from discharging fully their key function of strategic direction.
(*Standards and Quality in Education* The annual report of HM Chief Inspector of Schools, 1994)

If your governing body has been working together with the staff through the exercises suggested in this book it should be more effective than before, governor–teacher relationships will have been enhanced and, most important of all, the governors and staff together will be on their way to making their school more effective. In the last chapter we looked at the effectiveness of the school and in this final chapter we turn to a consideration of the effectiveness of the governing body. A governing body could approach this task in the same way that school effectiveness was discussed – that is, by devising its own criteria of effectiveness and then deciding upon and gathering the evidence required to show that the governing body is meeting those criteria. Alternatively, and particularly if time is limited, the criteria included later in this chapter could be used as a starting point or there could be a combination of the two approaches. Yet another way of tackling this issue is to ask some or all of the staff and some or all of the parents in which areas they think the governing body is most effective and in which areas it is least effective. Staff and parents might, for instance, be asked how many governors they feel they could identify from a group photograph – the results may be rather depressing! Parental opinion on the governors' annual report to parents and the subsequent meeting might also be sought, as could staff views on the effectiveness of governors' visits to the school. Other aspects of the work of the governing body could also be explored.

Included at the end of this chapter is a pro forma for the Governing Body Development Plan which could be completed after evaluation of the effectiveness of the governing body. A Plan such as this would set out the priorities for development of the governing body for, say, the next 12 months, and it could be linked to the School Development Plan as suggested in the previous chapter.

Determining the effectiveness of your governing body (Method 1)

The first step in evaluating its level of success is for the governing body to draw up its own criteria of effectiveness.

TASK 6.1 WHAT DO WE MEAN BY AN EFFECTIVE GOVERNING BODY?

This Task could be undertaken by the whole governing body or by a sub-group of governors or by governors and teachers together. It will probably take between 30 and 45 minutes.

List the criteria by which you would wish the effectiveness of your governing body to be judged. Once you have completed the list, look at the set of criteria and indicators which are set out later in this chapter and modify your list if you wish.

Once the criteria have been listed, the next step, in exactly the same way that school effectiveness was approached, is to decide upon what evidence might be needed in order to discover whether or not the governing body is fulfilling the criteria. It is also necessary to decide where that evidence might be found.

TASK 6.2 HOW CAN WE FIND OUT IF OUR GOVERNING BODY IS BEING EFFECTIVE?

This Task could be undertaken by the same group which carried out Task 6.1 and could immediately follow it. This Task will take about the same time, that is between 30 and 45 minutes. The two Tasks together could probably be completed in a two-hour training session, allowing for a coffee break in between them.

For each of the criteria of governing body effectiveness decided upon in Task 6.1, list the evidence which would be required to show that the governing body was meeting the criteria and where it might be found.

As with the discussion on school effectiveness in the last chapter, having decided upon the evidence which the governors wish to produce in order to satisfy themselves that they are meeting their own criteria of effectiveness, the next stage is to collect that evidence. This process will probably not take as long as it may have done to produce the evidence on the effectiveness of the school. Let us suppose, for instance, that one of the criteria decided upon is whether the governing body has a clear definition of its role. Provided that the governors are satisfied that they have discussed this issue and that a definition exists somewhere – perhaps in the school brochure or in the minutes of a meeting – it is not actually necessary to produce the document.

TASK 6.3 GATHERING THE EVIDENCE ON THE EFFECTIVENESS OF THE GOVERNING BODY

This Task could be undertaken by some or all of the governors. The time taken will depend upon the range of data to be collected.

Collect the necessary evidence, or discover where it is to be found, in order to assure the governors that they are meeting their criteria of effectiveness.

Just as the collection of the data on school effectiveness led to a discussion as to where and how the school might be made more effective, so, once the data on the effectiveness of the governing body has been collected, that evidence should be reviewed and discussed in order to ascertain where and how the effectiveness of the governing body can be increased.

TASK 6.4 HOW EFFECTIVE IS OUR GOVERNING BODY?

This Task should almost certainly be carried out by the whole governing body. The discussion could last up to an hour and will lead, where necessary, to the identification of areas for development.

Review the evidence which has been collected and decide how far your governing body is meeting the criteria of effectiveness which you decided upon. Where necessary note deficiencies and plan changes which will lead to improvement.

Determining the effectiveness of your governing body (Method 2)

The criteria which follow have been designed to help school governing bodies to evaluate their own effectiveness and to assist them in highlighting possible areas for development. The material, although in a slightly different format, has been used with a large number of governing bodies and is a simple way of helping governors to clarify their ideas on effectiveness and to identify areas for development. A two-hour session has been found long enough to work through the material in the manner suggested. Someone from outside the governing body can be a useful leader for the exercise, but this is not essential. Six criteria are proposed by which the effectiveness of a governing body is to be judged. Each of these criteria, which are very broad and general statements, is accompanied by a number of indicators which are much more specific and precise. The governors may, if they wish, add further criteria with associated indicators.

The governors are invited to indicate where evidence might be found to show that the governing body is meeting each of the indicators, though there is no need to have the evidence actually present. Such evidence might be found in documents – terms of reference for sub-groups, minutes of meetings, etc. – or alternatively through verbal evidence about the way in which the governing body is working. Governors can work in pairs and in order to save time pairs of governors may be asked to start at different points so that the first pair of governors is asked to begin with Criterion 1 before going on to Criterion 2, while the second pair starts with Criterion 2, the third pair with Criterion 3, and so on. At this stage the governors are asked only to satisfy themselves, if possible, that the governing body meets the various indicators. In this way all the criteria can be dealt with in about half an hour. At the end of this period, each pair of governors is asked in turn to go through the criterion with which they started. They are asked to identify *any gaps* which they found – that is, any indicator for which they were unable to find evidence of the governing body meeting that part of the criterion. These gaps should be recorded, preferably on a flip-chart for all to see. At this stage other governors may be able to provide evidence which fills in some of the gaps and it may be helpful for the group to read the 'Points for consideration', set out after the six criteria.

Now might be the time for a short break before the governors consider what action is required to fill in the gaps in order to enhance their effectiveness with regard to each of the criteria. For example, if the governing body does not have a clear set of aims (Criterion 2, Indicator (a)), perhaps time might be set aside at the next meeting of the governing body for discussion and agreement upon such aims. Once all the possible steps have been listed (and there may be a number of suggestions for each criterion) it may be necessary to establish priorities, particularly if there are many suggestions. Remember that if one tries to have too many priorities one ends up with no priorities! At this stage the governors' development plan pro forma might be completed, which will set out the steps to be taken in order to carry the process forward .

The six criteria which distinguish the effective governing body are, in summary, that it

1. works in partnership with the staff

2. works as an effective team

3. manages its business efficiently

4. fulfils its legal obligations

5. is concerned to promote school improvement

6. forms an effective link between the school and the community.

A governing body working in this way has a clear view of its role, a view which is shared by the staff. Individual governors know their school and are known, respected and trusted by the staff. There is a clear pattern of delegation with the headteacher and staff being clearly responsible for the day-to-day management of the school. Good communication systems ensure that all governors are kept fully informed. Above all, the governing body is concerned with school improvement. In order to do this effectively the governing body concentrates upon broad issues and forward planning and is involved, with the staff, in the ongoing monitoring processes of the work of the school.

The effective governing body: a set of criteria

Criterion 1 The governing body works in partnership with the staff

Indicators

(a) Governors and staff have arrived at an agreed statement of the school's aims and objectives.

(b) Governors are frequent and welcome visitors to the school.

(c) There is mutual trust and respect between governors and staff.

(d) Governors have a basic understanding of the school's curriculum and the variety of teaching and learning styles used in the school.

(e) Governors are kept informed about educational developments and are involved in discussions about curriculum policies.

(f) Governors are aware of the way in which the school is managed.

Criterion 2 The governing body works as an effective team

Indicators

(a) The governing body has a clear and agreed set of aims.

(b) Appropriate leadership is displayed.

(c) Contributions by individual governors are valued.

(d) There are clear and agreed delegation arrangements.

(e) Any sub-groups of the governing body have clear terms of reference and report back to the full governing body.

(f) Every governor contributes to the work of the governing body.

(g) There is an effective induction programme for newly appointed governors.

Criterion 3 The governing body manages its business effectively

Indicators

(a) All governors come fully prepared to meetings.

(b) There is a clear purpose to meetings.

(c) The agendas for meetings are well-planned and allow time for discussion of key issues. Supporting papers are well written and distributed in good time.

(d) The setting for meetings is comfortable and encourages contributions from individual governors.

(e) The manner in which the meetings are conducted encourages individual contributions.

(f) Meetings are of a reasonable length.

(g) Minutes of meetings are a clear, concise and accurate record and indicate what has to be done, by whom and by when.

(h) The governing body monitors its own performance.

Criterion 4 The effective governing body fulfils its legal obligations

Indicators

The governing body

(a) Meets at least once a term;

(b) Elect its Chair annually;

(c) Ensures that any committees with delegated powers are properly constituted;

(d) Has considered the LEA's statement on the curriculum;

(e) Has made appropriate arrangements for religious education and daily collective worship for the pupils;

(f) Has a policy on the provision of sex education in the school;

(g) Has a policy on provision for children with special educational needs;

(h) Decides upon the school's annual budget;

(g) Makes appropriate arrangements for staff appointments;

(i) Has in place policies relating to staff pay and discipline and grievance with

appropriate committees;
(j) Operates an equal opportunities policy;
(k) Prepares an annual report for parents and holds a meeting at which that report is discussed;
(l) Ensures the health and safety of adults and children on the school site.

NOTE: This list is not intended to be exhaustive. Governors should consult an up-to-date volume of *School Governors: A Guide to the Law*, published by the DFE.

Criterion 5 *The governing body is concerned to promote school improvement*

Indicators

(a) Governors have an awareness of what constitutes an effective school and of the factors which contribute towards school effectiveness.
(b) The governing body is concerned to promote a climate of school improvement.
(c) The governing body concentrates upon strategic planning and is appropriately involved in the production of the School Development Plan.
(d) The governing body ensures that the budget reflects the priorities established in the School Development Plan.
(e) Governors work with staff in an ongoing monitoring and evaluation of progress.
(f) High priority is given to staff and governor development.

Criterion 6 *The effective governing body forms an effective link between school and community*

Indicators

(a) The governors' annual report to parents is attractive, readable and seeks to encourage parental involvement.
(b) Governors actively encourage parents to attend the annual meeting.
(c) Governors actively seek to meet and talk with parents.
(d) The governing body communicates effectively with the LEA (non-grant-maintained schools only).
(e) Governors actively seek to promote the best interests of their schools within the community.

Points for consideration after seeking evidence relating to each of the indicators

Most of the indicators linked to the six criteria are quite self-explanatory but the following amplification may help in discussion of some of the issues.

1(b) In an ideal situation *every* governor would be a frequent and welcome visitor to the school but one must recognise that other commitments may prevent some from visiting the school as often as they would like. The governing body should ensure that such governors are somehow kept in touch with what is happening in the school. The use of the word 'welcome' is deliberate; some governors may visit frequently without their visits being welcomed by the staff! Would it be helpful for the governing body in consultation with the staff to draw up a set of guidelines for governors' visits to the school? (see chapter 3)

1(d) and (e) The curriculum is the whole range of learning experiences provided by the school for the children. The central purpose of the school is to provide that curriculum and all else is secondary to that purpose. Governors, if they are to play their proper part, must therefore have some knowledge of the curriculum in their school and have opportunities to discuss changes and developments in the curriculum.

1(f) The management structure will of course depend upon the size of the school. A very small primary school may have little or no formal structure whilst a large secondary school may have a relatively complex structure with a number of teachers holding posts of responsibility.

2(a) The aims of the *school* should not be confused with those of the *governing body*; they will be complementary but not identical. The aims of the school will concentrate upon outcomes for the pupils. The aims for a governing body will demonstrate what the governors are trying to achieve in order to underpin the aims of the school. For example, an aim of the governing body might be to ensure that all the resources available to the school are deployed to ensure the maximum benefit to all the pupils.

2(b) The use of the word 'leadership' rather than 'chairmanship' is deliberate. It is the work of the governing body, not the work of the Chair, which is being discussed here. In an effective governing body, every governor may offer leadership of the group at one time or another. The style of the leadership should be appropriate to the situation.

2(d) and (e), also 4(c) Is the governing body clear about exactly what powers have been delegated and to whom? Are those to whom power has been delegated equally clear about when they must refer back to the governing body? Many governing bodies have established sub-groups for dealing, for instance, with financial and personnel matters. This can be very effective and efficient provided that the groups have clear and agreed terms of reference. It is important, however, to ensure that all the governors are kept aware of the decisions being made by these groups and that membership of the groups is not restricted to the 'favoured few'.

N.B. Sub-groups of the governing body are *essential* to operate the agreed pay policy and to hear any disciplinary/grievance cases.

3 (a) to (g) The meetings of the full governing body are very important occasions; they are, after all, the only times at which all the governors meet together. It is therefore vital that everything possible should be done to make these meetings as effective and efficient as possible. The governors should ensure that the majority of their time is spent discussing the really important issues affecting their school. This may mean some self-discipline on the part of some governors!

5(c) A major aspect of the role of the governing body is forward planning. The School Development Plan (SDP) should be the central planning document for the coming year, setting out the school's priorities for development. Everything else – the budget, the staff inservice training programme, etc. – should be linked to the SDP. Within the SDP, there might well be a 'governors' development plan' setting out targets and priorities for the governing body in the coming year. Ways of involving governors in the production of the SDP have been fully discussed in chapter 5.

Once the governing body has reached some conclusions about its own effectiveness (no matter by what criteria that effectiveness is judged) and has decided where development is required, the Governors' Development Plan pro forma should be completed.

TASK 6.5 DRAWING UP A GOVERNORS' DEVELOPMENT PLAN
This is a Task best undertaken by the governing body as a whole.

Complete the Governors' Development Plan pro forma. Make arrangements to review progress towards achievement of the goals set out in that Plan.

GOVERNING BODY DEVELOPMENT PLAN PRO FORMA

Name of School...

Priorities for action	What has to be done (include targets/criteria)	By whom	By when	Progress Review
1				
2				
3				
4				
5				

Further Reading

Basics for School Governors by Joan Sallis, published by the Network Educational Press in 1993.

A short introduction to the role and responsibilities of governors which will be found invaluable by new governors.

Creating the Conditions for School Improvement: a handbook of staff development activities by Ainscow, Hopkins, Southworth and West, published by David Fulton Publishers in 1994.

This book, based on experience of working with improving schools, has a chapter on the involvement of staff, parents, pupils and governors and includes training material which may be photocopied and used by the purchaser.

Development Planning: a Practical Guide. Advice to governors, headteachers and teachers, published by the Department of Education and Science in 1991.

As its title indicates this is a practical guide to the vital business of School Development Planning. As such it will be particularly helpful to governors who may have little experience of this work.

Effective Management in Schools. A report for the Department for Education via the School Management Task Force Professional Working Party. HMSO, 1993.

This report is based upon the study of the management practice in 12 schools of differing types. Includes a chapter entitled 'The community, governors and the Local Education Authority'.

Good Management in Small Schools: a good practice guide for locally managed small schools. DFE, 1993.

A most helpful booklet especially but not exclusively for those involved in the management of small schools. Includes a section on the role of the governing body and, more unusually, on the role of the school secretary.

Heads and Governors: Building the Partnership by Joan Sallis, published by AGIT in 1994.

This book, as its title suggests, focuses upon the essential partnership between governors and headteacher.

Improving Schools, published by OFSTED in 1994.

Should be required reading for every headteacher, senior member of staff and at least one governor on every governing body. This most helpful booklet draws out some valuable lessons on school improvement based upon case studies of schools which *have* improved.

Moving to Management by Angela Thody, published by David Fulton Publishers in 1992.

This book looks at some of the roles of the governing body including financial and personnel management.

Planning for School Development: Advice to Governors and Teachers, published by the DES in 1989.

This was the first official booklet on development planning and contains many useful ideas. It could be read in conjunction with *Development Planning: A Practical Guide.*

School Governing Bodies: Making Progress by Peter Earley, published by the National Foundation for Educational Research (NFER) in 1994.

This is a report on a national survey of governors carried out by the National Foundation for Educational Research (NFER) in 1993/4. It includes an analysis of the composition of governing bodies, their operation and training and governors' ideas on what constitutes an effective governing body.

School Governors: A Guide to the Law, published and regularly updated by the DFE.

Every governor should have an up-to-date copy of this booklet.

School Governors: Leaders or Followers? edited by Angela Thody, published by Longman in 1994.

A collection of essays which looks at the issues of accountability and democracy as related to school governing bodies.

School Governors: What Governors Need to Know by Jeff Jones, Volumes 1, 2 and 3, published by David Fulton Publishers in 1993.

Three booklets packed with information on a wide range of topics from Assessment to Special Educational Needs.

The Empowered School: the management and practice of development planning by Hargreaves and Hopkins, published by Cassell in 1991.

Another very useful guide for schools wishing to improve their planning practice. It incorporates and develops the ideas set out in the two booklets published by the DES on this topic.

The New School Governor: Realizing the Authority in the Head and Governing Body by Holt and Hinds, published by Kogan Page in 1994.

This book looks at some of the political background to the recent changes in the educational system in the United Kingdom and examines in particular the issues of autonomy and accountability as they affect governing bodies.

The School Governors' Handbook by Martin Leonard, published by Blackwell in 1989.

A very useful introduction to the role and duties of governors.

The School Governors' Legal Guide by Chris Lowe, published by Croner and currently in its fifth edition.

A relatively expensive but invaluable reference book. Governing bodies which cannot afford a copy of their own may be able to borrow a copy from their LEA when necessary.

Towards Effective Partnerships in School Governance by Baginsky, Baker and Cleave, published by the National Foundation for Educational Research (NFER) in 1991.

This useful volume reports upon a research project in which the views of governors and headteachers were sought on a number of issues including the role of the governing body and relationships between governors and the school.

Working with Governors in Schools by Cynthia Beckett, Les Bell and Chris Rhodes, published by the Open University Press in 1991.

Another book which focuses upon the governor–headteacher relationship. It includes a list of 'Things to do' at the end of each chapter.

Index

action plans 65
advice and support 11
agenda for meetings 39
aims 18

Belbin, M. 21
brainstorm 6

Callaghan, J. 53
chair of governors 9, 23, 40
characteristics of effective schools 58
committee 46
communication 23
conflict 24
criteria for effective governing bodies 70, 73
criteria for effective schools 52 (*et seq.*)
curriculum 2, 48

decision making 41
delegation 43 (*et seq.*)
Department for Education (DFE) 8, 75

Education Acts
  1944 48
  1986 42, 43
  1988 48
  1993 49
effective
  governing bodies 4, 69 (*et seq.*)
  schools 52 (*et seq.*)
  teams 17 (*et seq.*)
expectations 27

flip-chart 27

governors and curriculum 48 (*et seq.*)
governors
   contributing to school effectiveness 59
   'corner' 31, 32
   development plan 12, 68, 73, 77
   introduction of new 18
   involvement in planning 68
   'of the month' 31, 33
   report to parents 14
   responsibilities 9
   role 10 (*et seq.*)
   training 5, 61
   visits to school 3, 33 (*et seq.*), 49
governor-staff relationships 26 (*et seq.*)
   enhancing 31
   factors affecting 28
governing body
   and incompetent teachers 30
   effective 4, 23, 69 (*et seq.*)
   managing business of 38 (*et seq.*), 74
   responsibilities 1, 8, 74

headteacher 8, 13, 14, 29
   report to governors 42

knowledge of school by governors 10, 34 (*et seq.*)

Managing Schools Today 22
meetings 38 (*et seq.*)
mentor 18
monitoring 13, 63

National Curriculum 48

Office for Standards in Education (OFSTED) 1, 13, 53–4, 64

parents 14, 55, 69
parent-governors 14
parents meeting 15
partnership 3, 9, 73

planning 12, 62 (*et seq.*)
priorties in planning 64
promoting the school 15

religious education 45, 48

school-community links 13, 75
school development planning 62 (*et seq.*)
school improvement 60
sex education 45, 49
special educational needs (SEN) 49

teachers 2, 12
    incompetent 30
teacher-governors 29
teamwork 12, 17 (*et seq.*), 74
team
    composition 21
    development 24
    effective 17, 20, 74
Times Educational Supplement 15
training 5
Tuckman, W. B. 24

visits to school 3, 33 (*et seq.*), 49

working parties 46